CHRISTENDOM
and the
NATIONS

JAMES B. JORDAN

BOOKS

AN IMPRINT OF ATHANASIUS PRESS

CHRISTENDOM AND THE NATIONS
By James B. Jordan, Th.M.

Copyright © 2018 Theopolis Books
An Imprint of Athanasius Press

Athanasius Press
715 Cypress Street
West Monroe, Louisiana 71291
www.athanasiuspress.org

ISBN: 978-0-9862924-9-1 (softcover)

All rights reserved. No part of this publication may be reproduced, stored in a retrieval system, or transmitted in any form or by any means—electronic, mechanical, photocopy, recording, or any other—except for brief quotations in printed reviews, without the prior permission of the publisher.

TABLE OF CONTENTS

Preface   *v*

1. The Origin of the Nations   *1*

2. National Integrity   *17*

3. Global Unity   *31*

4. International Relations   *45*

5. National Boundaries   *57*

6. International Alliances   *71*

7. United States Foreign Policy: Some Observations   *89*

8. International Communications   *105*

9. The United Nations   *115*

10. Sanctuary   *129*

11. The Sanctuary Movement and the Immigration Problem   *141*

12. A Christian Foreign Polity   *155*

Bibliography   *164*

Preface

This book was originally written in 1987 as part of the Biblical Blueprints series published by the Institute for Christian Economics. After my manuscript had been completed, the editor of this series, Gary North, determined that each book should employ the "five-point covenant model." He believed, perhaps rightly, that if each volume used the same biblical structure it would be easier for readers to acquire a useful and transportable biblical model for dealing with issues. Whatever the case, my manuscript employs a different, three-part biblical model, so it no longer could be published in this series. The rights were returned to me, and I self-published it as *The Bible and the Nations*.[1]

In 1992, most of the chapters were serialized in a small short-lived Dutch periodical, *Symbiotica*, under the title, "Christianity and International Relations."

The original version of this material was written when the Soviet Union still posed the greatest visible threat to Christian order. By 1992 this was no longer the case, and I rewrote some of the material at that time. Now it is 2017, and the world has changed a great deal. I have no intention

---

1 James B. Jordan, *The Bible and the Nations* (Niceville, Fla.: Biblical Horizons, 1987).

of rewriting this material a third time. I believe that the principles set forth herein remain of value, and that there is little to be gained by trying to update the details.

James B. Jordan
Pentecost 2017

The Origin of the Nations

And He made from one man every nation of mankind to live on all the face of the earth, having determined their appointed times and the boundaries of their habitation
— Acts 17:26 (New American Standard Bible)

INTRODUCTION

In giving His great commission to His disciples, the Lord Jesus Christ spoke in terms not of individuals, nor yet of families, but of nations:

> All authority in heaven and on earth has been given to Me. Go, therefore, and make disciples of all the nations, baptizing them in the name of the Father and the Son and the Holy Spirit, teaching them to [h]follow all that I commanded you; and behold, I am with you [i]always, to the end of the age. (Matt. 28:18-20, NASB)

Nations are made up of people, and it is people who are baptized and taught, yet Jesus says that the goal of all this baptizing and teaching is that the nations should be discipled. This has always been the view of the Church.

There were Christian nations and non-Christian nations. Christian nations were nations that (1) recognized the sanctity of the visible or institutional Church, and (2) lived by Christian moral values. Non-Christian nations were nations that did not recognize the Church and did not live by Christian values.

Today, however, we hear from many evangelical writers that there is no such thing as a Christian nation. The United States and the nations of Europe, we are told, were never Christian nations.

Indeed, there cannot be such a thing as a Christian political order. The proponents of this view insist that Christianity cannot disciple the nations and that there cannot be a Christian nation. There can only be Christian churches, hiding in pagan/secular nations, waiting for the end of the world. They maintain that the Church has always been wrong when she tried to disciple the nations. They criticize Constantine for making the Roman Empire Christian. They magnify the problems of the Crusades, using them as examples of "what happens when you try to have a Christian state." They criticize Martin Luther, John Calvin, the Puritans, and the Reveil for trying to reform society.

Yet this is far from historic, orthodox Christianity. No Christian tradition has ever held such notions, not the Eastern Orthodox, not the Roman Catholic, and not the Protestant. Only a tiny handful of drop-out sects, like the Mennonites, have ever denied that the nations can and should be discipled—or that at least Jesus should find us trying to disciple them when He comes back.

After all, are we to disciple the family? Then why not the state? Biblical Christianity claims that all areas of life are claimed by Christ the King, and all must answer to Him. There is a kind of Christianization that is appropriate to the state and another kind appropriate to the individual.

A Christian state is one that conforms to the principles of Divine law and recognizes the sanctity of the Church. A Christian Church is one that properly administers Word and sacraments. A Christian person is one who is faithful in life. These are different ways in which the rule of Christ is made manifest in the various spheres of life.

In these studies, then, we are concerned with discipling the nations. First of all, we have to discern from Scripture what a *nation* is. Then we need to look at principles that help us understand the purpose of the nations in history according to God's plan. Finally, we need to take up some modern problem areas in international relations that the Bible can help us address.

My credentials are those of a theologian, not of an expert in international relations. Thus, it would be presumptuous of me to fill these essays with detailed suggestions to the rulers of today's nations. At the same time, however, there is clearly a need for biblical and theological foundations to be set out, to stimulate Christian reflection in this area. It is my hope and prayer that these essays will provide those foundations and that stimulus.

WHAT IS A NATION?

In these essays we are concerned with what the Bible and the Christian faith have to say about "international relations." For the most part, we are talking about relations between social/legal entities called *nations*, but before we can talk about international relations, we need to have some idea of what a *nation* is.

The *Random House Dictionary of the English Language*[2] gives two definitions of *nation* that are relevant to this study. It says that a nation is "a body of people, associated with a

---

[2] *Random House Dictionary of the English Language*, Edited by Jess Stein and Laurence Urdang (New York, N.Y.: Random House, 1967).

particular territory, that is sufficiently conscious of its unity to seek or to possess a government peculiarly its own." The second definition is, "an aggregation of persons of the same ethnic family, often speaking the same language or cognate languages."[3]

We may notice here are four ideas mixed up in the idea of *nation*. They are: geographical location, government, ethnicity, and language.

The same kind of mixture of ideas is seen in the original dictionary of Noah Webster. He writes that a *nation* is "a body of people inhabiting the same country, or united under the same sovereign or government; as the English *nation*; the French *nation*. It often happens that many nations are subject to one government; in which case, the word *nation* usually denotes a body of people speaking the same language, or a body that has formerly been under a distinct government, but has been conquered, or incorporated with a larger nation. Thus the empire of Russia comprehends many nations, as did formerly the Roman and Persian empires. *Nation*, as its etymology imports, originally denoted a family or race of men descended from a common progenitor [cp. 'native'—JBJ], like *tribe*, but by emigration, conquest, and intermixture of men of different families, this distinction is in most countries lost."[4]

The important thing to learn from Webster's definition is that a *state* or *government* is not the same thing as a *nation*. The state of the U.S.S.R. until recently ruled over several nations or peoples, for example: Lithuania, Latvia, Estonia, Russia, Byelorussia, the Ukraine, Armenia, Moldova, Georgia, Azerbaijan, Kyrgyzstan, Kazakhstan, Uzbekistan,

---

3 Ibid.

4 Noah Webster, *An American Dictionary of the English Language:: Intended to Exhibit, I. The Origin, Affinities and Primary Signification of English Words, As Far As They Have Been Ascertained; II. the Genuine Orthography and Pronunciation of Words, According to General* (New York, N.Y.: S. Converse, Hezekiah Howe, 1828).

Turkmenistan, and Tajikistan. Each of these represents a separate and distinct nation or people, but all were ruled by one tyrannical imperial state that called itself a republic.

We should note right here that the Bible is concerned with *nations* far more than with *states*. States or governments come and go, but the peoples to whom God has apportioned the earth abide from generation to generation. As Christians, we must think primarily in terms of nations and peoples and only secondarily in terms of states or governments.

But we need to return to our exploration of what a nation is. Switzerland is a nation with four languages. Some Swiss Cantons speak German, some French, some Italian, and one Romansh. Yet, Switzerland is not four nations ruled by one overpowering state. It is one nation. The people all regard themselves as Swiss. What is it about the Swiss that makes them a nation, since it is not a common language? I think that upon reflection we can come up with three factors. One is geography. All the Swiss live in the same general place, and that place (the Swiss Alps) is relatively isolated from other places. Second is race. All the Swiss are Europeans, though some are Germanic and some are South European. Third, and I think most important, is religion. All Swiss are officially Christian, though some are Lutheran, some Calvinistic, and some Roman Catholic.

Yet, the Italian Swiss don't want to leave Switzerland and join Italy, nor do the French Swiss want to join France, nor do the German Swiss want to join Germany. Why not? The reason is not language. Nor is it geography, because there are Alpine areas in France, Italy, and Germany. Superficially, it is not religion, since the Italian Swiss are Roman Catholics and we might think they would be more at home in Italy. Looking deeper, however, the difference between the Swiss and the nations around them turns out to be religion. Switzerland has a distinctive culture that has been influenced by Calvinism or "Reformed" Christianity. Even though many of the people are not Calvinists but Lutherans or Roman Catholics, all have been *influenced* by Calvinism.

Culture is a product of religion, and the reason the Swiss feel themselves to be different from other nations is because of their religiously formed cultural patterns.

The United States is very much like Switzerland. Until recently, the U.S. has been relatively isolated from the rest of the world by geography. The U.S. has been a melting pot of various races and of various forms of Christianity. The great internal tensions that have arisen in American history have come from her growth pains as a *nation*; that is, as a real community of people.

While the War Between the States was fought partially over tariffs, it was also fought over the place of black people within the nation. Even after the War, North and South handled this problem differently. A nationwide resolution of the legal status of black people was not imposed until the Civil Rights Movement of the 1960s and later. Just as Switzerland came into existence as various peoples learned to live in community, the same process is seen in the United States as regards immigrants and especially blacks.

A common geographical location is almost always necessary for a body of people to consider itself a nation—but not always.

The Jews are the premier example here. For almost two millennia, the Jews possessed no specific homeland, yet they were definitely a nation. Jews were scattered in communities and "ghettoes" in many nations, but they always saw themselves as Jews first. Their religious covenant took precedent over their geographical location. By the way, the Jews are *not* united by race. During the early Middle

Ages, the Turkic nation of Khazars converted to Judaism. Many modern Jews are racially from other groups. The unifying factor is *religion* (covenant), not race.[5]

There is no other example like the Jews, though under some temporary periods of time, we can see similar sentiments among other peoples. Many French Canadians feel closer to France than to the rest of Canada, which is English by culture. Thus, there has been a "Free Quebec" movement in recent years, and Charles de Gaulle (of European France) was hailed as a hero by many French Canadians when he visited them and ended a speech with the war cry: "Vive le Quebec libre!" Over the long haul, however, such nationalistic sentiment will undergo significant changes. If Quebec ever separated from Canada, it would probably not join France and become part of that nation, but rather become a separate nation.

Drawing this together, we can say the following: *A nation is a body of people, usually living in the same place, sharing a common faith and culture, and desiring a common and separate government.* I say *desiring* a government because many nations have historically been under the oppression of conquering states. And I did not mention a common language, because as we have seen that is not always necessary.

In summary, the factors that enter into nationhood are:

- Religion as well as the customs, viewpoints, folk ways, and culture that stem from a particular religious worldview.
- Government, or the desire to have one's own governmental structures.
- Geography, except in rare circumstances.
- In some cases, ethnic and/or linguistic unity.

---

5 Arthur Koestler, *The Thirteenth Tribe* (New York, N.Y.: Random House, 1976).

NATION AND STATE

When we speak of "Christianity and the state," what do we mean? Throughout these essays we shall have to refer to the state as a political organization over against the nations, which as we have seen are religio-cultural organisms. Some reflection on what is meant by "the state" is needed at the outset.

The Random House Dictionary of the English Language gives this definition to the word state: "the body politic as organized for civil rule and government (distinguished from church)."[6] The reason why some reflection on this definition is needed is that when we speak of the state, or of church-state relations, we generally do not stop to remember that there is no such thing as the state. The word state is an abstract noun, and it refers to people-as-organized-and-ruled-politically. What actually exists is not the state, but people. Particularly, what actually exists are certain people who rule over other people: civil magistrates. To treat an abstract idea as if it were an existing thing is the logical error of hypostatization or reification.

According to logician S. Morris Engel, "The State can do no wrong. Only persons, not 'the State,' can be said to do right or wrong."[7] The Bible does not speak of the state, but of magistrates, judges, elders, and kings—in other words, of *persons*. Practically speaking, when we speak of the *state* or of "the states of modern Europe," we are speaking of a geographical area governed by certain rulers.

What kind of rule is involved? Not moral suasion, but force is the defining rule of the magistrate. Romans 13 describes civil magistrates as rulers who govern by the

---

6 *Random House Dictionary of the English Language*, Stein and Urdang.

7 S. Morris Engel, *With Good Reason: An Introduction to Informal Fallacies* (New York, N.Y.: St. Martin's Press, 1976), 57.

sword and who collect taxes to finance their government. To this conception of the state, we need only add the notion of a geographical boundary maintained by force.

It is important for us to bear in mind that political relationships, and thus international relationships, always boil down to *personal* interactions. When the United States gives foreign aid to Ethiopia, for instance, what is really happening (in the concrete, real world) is that civil magistrates in the United States have collected money and goods from the American people through taxation. These American rulers then pass these monies and goods to the ruling magistrates in Ethiopia. In other words, the foreign aid is not going from state to state, because there is no such thing as a state. Nor is the foreign aid going from the American people to the Ethiopian people. Rather, it is going from American rulers to Ethiopian rulers, provided such rulers do what the Americans giving them money tell them to do. When we think clearly about this, we see why there tends to be so much corruption in the foreign aid programs set up by the United States.

A *state*, then, is a geographical area governed by magistrates through the use of force. Ideally, such civil governments should correspond to nations as cultural units. Historically, however, very often powerful men use the weapons of force to create *states* whose boundaries have nothing to do with the natural boundaries of the nations.

THE ORIGIN OF THE NATIONS

Does God want there to be many nations? The present state of affairs shows that He does, at least in some sense. God is in control of history, and so our present diversity of nations reflects His supreme plan for our good. But, is this diversity of nations a result of sin? If man had not sinned, would there be this "division of powers?" Is there something unfortunate about there being many different nations and languages? Is this an undesirable state of affairs, one that God wants us to overcome?

Not at all. The diversity of nations and even of languages is part of God's creation design. In Genesis 2, before the Fall of man, God had already apportioned the earth into various geographical zones. There was the land of Eden, with its Garden in the east. But there were also the lands of Havilah, Cush, and Assyria, watered by the rivers Pishon, Gihon, and Hiddekel (Gen. 2:11-14). Now, while Moses (or whoever put Genesis in its final shape) may have pulled these *names* from later history, the actual *lands* were set up by creation design.

Most Christians are used to thinking that God created the nations by scattering people at the Tower of Babel. Not so. The curse of Babel came because the people *rejected* God's plan of diversified nations. God had to come down and force them to do what He intended for them. Notice that it is in Genesis 10 that we have listed the seventy nations of the world. The story of the Tower of Babel is not recorded until Genesis 11.

God is Three Persons and yet also One God, and His world should reflect His Oneness and His Threeness—His Divine unity and His Divine diversity. God has established different colors and races of people, different sizes and shapes, different languages, musics, and dances. For the Christian, unity and diversity are not in conflict with one another, because God is Three and One.

Let us look now at the story of the Tower of Babel. We read first of all, "Now all the earth used the same language and the same words." (Gen. 11:1, NASB). The word translated *language* in this verse actually means *lip*. The phrase "same words" (sometimes translated "speech") refers to language, but the phrase "one lip" refers to religion.

For instance, commenting on the Tower of Babel, the prophet Zephaniah wrote: "For then I will restore to the peoples pure lips, so that all of them may call on the name of the Lord" (Zeph. 3:9, NASB). The third and only other place in English Bibles where the Hebrew *lip* is mistranslated as "language" is Psalm 81:4-5, where again it clearly refers to religious confession, not to a foreign language: "For it is a *statute* for Israel, an *ordinance* of the God of Jacob. He established it as a *testimony* in Joseph when he went throughout the land of Egypt. I heard a *language* [lip] I did not know" (NASB, emphasis mine).

Notice that the word *language* is parallel to *statute*, *ordinance*, and *testimony* in the preceding phrases. It clearly refers to a religious confession, not just to Egyptian vocabulary and syntax.

A glance at a Bible concordance will show the religious meaning of *lip*. Start by looking at Job 27:4; 33:3; Psalm 12:2-4; 16:4; 40:9; 45:2; 51:15 ("Lord, open my lips, so that my mouth may declare Your praise," NASB); Isa. 6:5 ("Because I am a man of unclean lips, and I live among a people of unclean lips; for my eyes have seen the King, the Lord of armies," NASB); Isa. 6:7; and Mal. 2:6-7.

We have taken this little excursion into word study in order to show that what happened at the Tower of Babel was not first and foremost a division of languages, but rather a division of religious beliefs. The idea of speaking one language or another is not absolutely excluded from this word *lip* (see Isa. 19:18), but in the context of Genesis 11, there is clearly a difference between the "one lip" and "one speech" of verse one.

"And it came about, as they journeyed east [literally, eastward], that they found a plain in the land of Shinar and settled there," (Gen. 11:2, NASB). Just as Cain moved away from God by moving east (Gen. 4:6), so this "eastward" movement signifies movement away from God. The gathering of people in Genesis 11 was under the leadership of Nimrod, son of Cush, son of Ham (Gen. 10:6-12). According to these verses, Nimrod founded both Babylon and Nineveh (Assyria), the two great empires which God's chosen people must deal with later on.

> Then they said to one another, "Come, let's make bricks and fire them thoroughly." And they used brick for stone, and they used tar for mortar. And they said, "Come, let's build ourselves a city, and a tower whose top will reach into heaven, and let's make a name for ourselves; otherwise we will be scattered abroad over the face of all the earth." (Gen. 11:3-4, NASB)

God had told both Adam and Noah (Gen. 9:1) to spread out and fill the earth. Nimrod and his cohorts rejected God's plan. They did not want to build the city of God, slowly and gradually by faith. Rather, like Cain before them, they wanted an instant city, built on power and might.

Cain had built his city on the human sacrifice of his brother (Gen. 4), and Nimrod built his city (culture) and Tower (worship center) of *bricks*. When we remember that man is made of dust (Gen. 2:7), and that God's House is made of people, "living stones" (1 Pet. 2:4-8), we can see a double meaning in what we read here in Genesis 11. Nimrod's world of bricks cemented by asphalt served to symbolize his *unified society of men*, all stuck together in one place, not spreading out and shepherding the world.

These men knew that their Tower—probably a pyramid, a symbolic "holy mountain"—would not physically reach into heaven. It was a religious center that would enable them, as they thought, to storm the gates of heaven and seize the Tree of Life, from which men were excluded (Gen. 3:24). This is the goal of all pagan works-religion, and it was their goal as well.

We need to notice also that they wanted to make themselves a name. They did not want to be given a name by God, or wear His name. They wanted to make a name for themselves, to glorify themselves.

> Now Yahweh came down to see the city and the tower which the men had built. And the Lord said, "Behold, they are one people, and they all have the same language [lip, confession, ideology]. And this is what they have started to do, and now nothing which they plan to do will be impossible for them. Come, let Us go down and there confuse their language [lip, confession, ideology], so that they will not understand one another's speech [lip, confession, ideology]." (Gen. 11:5-7, NASB)

The author here pokes fun at the Tower of Babel. It was going to reach to heaven, but God had to "come down" just to even see it! Also, in Gen. 11:5, the author calls this bunch of rebels "sons of men." Like Adam and Eve, they wanted to make themselves gods, but they were nothing but mere men.

It is surprising to hear God say that because the people are unified, "nothing which they plan to do will be impossible for them." In one sense, we know that God can always stop men from doing anything, but the language used here points to the fact that in terms of the economy God has established in the world, there is strength in unity. God does not want the wicked to rule the world, so He moves to destroy their unity.

It is important to see that it was not a simple unity of language that gave these men power. Rather, they all thought the same way. They had a common ideology, a common religious faith. Without this anti-God unity, they could not have cooperated. In order to shatter this unity, God did not simply divide their languages. First and foremost, He shattered their ideologies.

What the story of the Tower of Babel tells us is that there was originally only one pagan, anti-God religion in the world. At the Tower of Babel, God acted to diversify paganism. All the heathen religions in the world have the same basic ideas, but each is slightly different from the rest. One group worships Thor and his kin, another Zeus and his family, another Jupiter and his cohorts. One nation pursues Baal, another Chemosh, another Molech, and another Amon-Ra. One group of revolutionary socialists follows Marx-and-Lenin, another follows Marx-and-Mao, another Marx-and-Castro, and another Marx-and-Ho Chi Minh. Still others follow Adolf Hitler. From the Christian point of view, there is little difference between these pagan religions, but from their point of view the differences are great. Each pagan nation has its own god, and wars are fought over them.

If it seems strange that God Himself would act to create these different pagan religions, we have to remember that according to Rom. 1:18-32, God punishes sin by giving people over to it. Idolatry is destructive to human life, and if men rebel against God, He will give them over to worse and worse forms of idolatry, until either they repent or are destroyed. The punishment fits the crime.

According to Gen. 11:1, all the people not only had a common ideology (lip), they also had the same language (speech). The passage clearly implies that God also confounded their languages so that they would not understand one another. As a result, not only were their religions in conflict, but they could not understand one another's speech either. Other peoples could not really speak; they could only bark like animals. The Greeks called them "bar-bar-ians." Nations viewed themselves as the only "human beings," and other peoples as something less, enslavable beasts.

As we shall see in these essays, God has established Christianity to create a true unity of confession (lip) among all nations and peoples, but this unity will not destroy the diversity of languages. Rather, each nation and language will praise Him in its own tongue (Rev. 7:9). Thus, the scattering of languages at the Tower of Babel was not a curse. Rather, it was the multiplication of pagan religions that showed God's judgment against the Tower-builders. Even here, however, the fact that *God will never permit non-Christians to form a world coalition again* is a blessing to Christians. No matter how hard they try, the pagan dream of a secular "united nations" is doomed to failure. It is the true faith that is destined to triumph in history.

CONCLUSION

Nations are not the same things as states or governments. They are organic social groupings of people. Usually a nation has a common language, but a nation always shares a common cultural outlook, stemming from religious presuppositions, and a nation always desires to govern itself. There are many nations because God is Three and yet One, and international diversity reflects His being. At the Tower of Babel, early man refused to carry out God's plan to diversify humanity, so God forced them to.

National Integrity

Now there were Jews residing in Jerusalem, devout men from every nation under heaven. And when this sound occurred, the crowd came together and they were bewildered, because each one of them was hearing them speak in his own language. They were amazed and astonished, saying, "Why, are not all these who are speaking Galileans? And how is it that we each hear them in our own language to which we were born?"
— Acts 2:5-8 (New American Standard Bible)

We have seen that God desires there to be many nations in the world, each Christian, each glorifying Him in its own way. God is One, but God is also "Many." The Christian faith, unlike every other religion, teaches that the One God exists in three distinct Persons. "The Father is God, the Son is God, and the Holy Spirit is God, and yet not three gods but One God," says the ancient Athanasian Creed. God not only exists in three Persons, but He also has many attributes.

Humanity was created in the very image of God, so there is a "oneness" and also a "manyness" to the human species. In this essay, we want to explore the implications of the "manyness" of humanity, as these relate to the question of the nations and their place in God's plan for history.

Each of the three Persons of the Godhead has *integrity*. The Father is not the Son. The Son is not the Spirit. The Spirit is not the Father. Each is a unique Person in God. We can have a personal relationship with each of them. Just so, each individual human being has personal integrity, though humanity as a whole is united (legally and genetically) in Adam, and redeemed humanity is united (legally and Spiritually) in Jesus Christ.

Similarly, Genesis 10 lists seventy nations. We are meant to understand that after the Tower of Babel, God diversified humanity into these seventy nations. Each nation reflected God's infinite character in a special way. Each nation had integrity and deserved respect as a separate and distinct nation.

Throughout the Bible, the number seventy is used as a symbol for the nations of the world. We shall see more about this later on in these essays. For now, we need to note that God's process of national diversification has continued down to the present day. There are far more than a mere seventy nations today, and this is part of God's plan. Since God is infinite, each new human being born into the world reflects His image in a new and uniquely different way. Similarly, the multiplication of nations and languages, of dances and musics, of dress and cuisine, simply serves to reflect God's infinite character in more and more splendid ways. So, let the nations multiply and increase, to the glory of our Triune God.

When the New Covenant arrived on the day of Pentecost, men from every nation heard the gospel in their own tongues. By this miracle, God affirmed the goodness and integrity of each language and nation under heaven. Modern secular humanism, however, acts to destroy this integrity by seeking to create a monolithic culture, imposed from the top down by the state.

The secular humanist wants to elevate the state (the ruler) over the nations and restructure the nations (peoples) in terms of abstract political designs. The biblical plan is quite the reverse. In the Bible, all the most important governmental functions are local—personal—well below the level of the nation itself. Such local governments always work to support national integrity and the cultural uniqueness of each of God's peoples. The pagan/humanist principle of big government always works to destroy the traditions and folkways of the nations.

The best recent example of this has been the Soviet Union. Officially, each Soviet "republic" had its own government, traditions, and leaders. In fact, the public displays of regional folk traditions were nothing more than a sop to the people. Only when these traditions were regarded as politically irrelevant were they allowed to exist.

SMALL-SCALE GOVERNMENT

In Judges 6, we find the Angel of Yahweh appearing to Gideon, the son of "Joash the Abiezrite" (Judg. 6:11). When God tells Gideon that he is to save Israel, Gideon protests, "My family is the least in Manasseh, and I am the youngest in my father's house" (Judg. 6:15, NASB). These verses, and many others like them in the Old Testament, show us the intensely local character of biblical government.

It is hard for us to imagine how small the land of Palestine really is. From Dan to Beersheba, the biblical expression for the length of the land, is only about 145 miles, for a total of about 10,000 square miles for the land. This is about the size of Vermont or New Hampshire. New Hampshire has ten counties, while Vermont has thirteen. Israel was divided among thirteen tribes (counties), since Manasseh was split into two groups.[8] The part of Manasseh from which Gideon

---

8 There were actually thirteen Israelite tribes, since Joseph's tribe

came was the largest of these thirteen "counties," measuring about 30 miles by 40 miles, about 1200 square miles, which is equivalent to a medium-sized county in the United States today.

What we note from Judges 6 is that people did not simply consider themselves as coming from Manasseh, but from smaller areas or towns within this tribe. Joash was an Abiezrite. In Israel, people identified themselves in terms of small localities, each one unique and precious in its own way. This points to the intensely local character of biblical government.

Another perspective on localism comes from Exodus 18. When Israel came out of Egypt, they were met by Godly Jethro, Moses' father-in-law. Jethro advised Moses to divide the nation into small units for governmental purposes. His plan is: "Furthermore, you shall select out of all the people able men who fear God, men of truth, those who hate dishonest gain; and you shall place these over them as leaders of thousands, of hundreds, of fifties, and of tens." (Exod. 18:21, NASB). The reference is not to ten persons but to ten households—all the same, a very small governmental unit.

Jethro advised that most matters should be handled at the local level, and only tough cases should be passed up the line through an appeal system: "Let them judge the people at all times; and let it be that they will bring to you every major matter, but they will judge every minor matter themselves. So it will be easier for you, and they will carry the burden

---

became two tribes: Ephraim and Manasseh. The tribe of Levi did not possess a county, however, but lived in Levitical cities all throughout the land. This makes for twelve counties.

The tribe of Manasseh, however, divided in half, with part living on each side of the Jordan. These came to be two separate counties. So, there were thirteen counties in Israel.

with you." (Exod. 18:22, NASB). Thus, all primary, day-to-day decisions would be made at the local level. Only a few matters would be of concern to larger units of government.

Localism in Church and state ensures that justice will be tempered with sympathy. When local churches and states are governed by people far away, true order is impossible. Local people know one another best. They have personal interaction. They understand one another's problems, and because they know each other, they can tell the difference between high-handed sins and sins of ignorance. They know who is poor and who is rebellious. They know how to deal firmly but charitably with one another.

AN EXAMPLE OF LOCALISM: THE UNITED STATES

Rousas J. Rushdoony has noted how the Christians in the United States imitated the biblical pattern in the area of local government. He writes, "It would be a serious error to assert that the alternative to federal sovereignty is State Rights. Important as the states are, they are not the basic unit of the American system. The basic unit is clearly and without question *the county*."

Rushdoony mentions three fundamental powers that are lodged at the county level.[10] First is the *property tax*. The power to tax property is the power to destroy and disinherit. Since local people control the election of tax assessors and county supervisors, the taxation of property seldom becomes oppressive. This prevents central governments from destroying the citizenry.

---

9 Rousas J. Rushdoony, *The Nature of the American System* (Nutley, N.J.: The Craig Press, 1965), 8-9.

10 Ibid., 9ff.

Second is *criminal law*. Law enforcement officers, police, and judges are officers of the county, not of the state. Until recent years, executions were held at the county seat. In a dramatic reversal, nowadays virtually no execution takes place without being appealed to the United States Supreme Court.

Third is *civil law*. Most civil law is county law, enforced by local courts by locally elected officials.

Thus, in the United States citizens are primarily under the government of local officials—or at least that is the way it was originally ordered. The history of the United States is a history of centralization. First the states began removing power from the local counties, and then the federal government began removing power from the states. As the U.S. has become more secular, it has become more statist.

Even so, the Christian heritage is still operative to a significant degree. In most countries of the world the police are accountable to the central state power. In America, the police are completely local. Rushdoony summarizes the local character of American police:

> 1. The police are a locally controlled and hence decentralized agency which is unrelated to other police bodies of other cities or counties and lacking in any national federation or union.
>
> 2. The police are not a military body, even if in uni-form. They are civilians in every sense of the word, and their authority is a civilian authority.
>
> 3. The police are supported by local property owners, whose agency they are, by means of a tax on property. The entire support of the police is local, and it is the property tax.
>
> 4. Their orientation is accordingly local, and the protection of life and property is their essential task. They are thus essentially a non-political body.

> 5. Police power is really in the hands of the citizenry, who retain the right to make citizen arrests. Thus, in America, the citizenry does not surrender police power to the police.[11]

To summarize: A Christian land will tend toward local government in both church and state, with higher levels of government acting only as courts of appeal. Only such matters that must by their very nature be handled at a higher level will be delegated to that higher level. Otherwise, fundamental government remains local.

LOCALISM AND THE NATIONS

We have already seen that nations (peoples) and states (civil governments) are not the same thing. In a biblical society, a nation would be composed of many local civil governments. For the most part, the nation would be the larger unit and the state would be the smaller unit. The national government would actually be built up from alliances among local governments.

In non-Christian philosophy, the exact reverse is true. The state as a political entity exercises power over a large area, often embracing several nations or peoples. Unity is not created by consensus but by force. Local officials do not really govern at all; instead, all they do is carry out the decisions made at distant higher levels.

This is most clearly seen in the empires of the ancient world. Every Bible reader is familiar with the fact that the Assyrian empire conquered Northern Israel and took the ten tribes into captivity. After this, the Assyrians moved other people into the holy land. "Then the king of Assyria brought people from Babylon, Cuthah, Avva, Hamath, and Sepharvaim, and settled them in the cities of Samaria in place of the sons of Israel. So they took possession of

---

11 Ibid., 159-60

Samaria and lived in its cities." (2 Kings 17:24, NASB). The remainder of 2 Kings 17 describes what happened to these foreign people: They became the Samaritans, who appear in the New Testament.

(A lot of speculation has surrounded the question of what happened to these "ten lost tribes." Some say they are the gypsies, others that they are the Anglo-Saxon peoples, and others that they are the American Indians. Actually, these tribes were not lost at all, but merged with the two southern tribes taken into captivity by Babylon later on. Representatives from all the tribes returned to the land eventually, after the captivity. For proof, see Luke 2:36: Anna was of the tribe of *Asher*, one of the ten "lost" tribes.)

A couple of centuries after the Assyrians took away the people of Northern Israel, the Babylonians under Nebuchadnezzar carried off the people of Judah into captivity. The books of Daniel and Ezekiel describe this captivity.

Now, what was going on here? It was the policy of these ancient empires to move whole populations of people from place to place, scattering them, so as to destroy national unity. The central planners of these empires wanted to break up all local ties and allegiances and make people loyal only to the central state, that is, to the imperial court and bureaucracy.

In non-Christian thought, the most important level of government is not local, but central. The centralized imperial state manipulates the nations (peoples) in order to destroy them. The Christian faith, committed to localism in the political realm, stands firmly against this.

MODERN PROBLEMS

The states of modern Europe are actually composed of several nations each. In recent years, these small nations have become insistent that they be allowed cultural diversity, and some have even demanded independence. This seems strange to us, because we are used to thinking of France, Spain, and Great Britain as single, unified nations, but they are not. In each case, the most powerful nation in these countries has conquered and subdued the others. This state-imposed unity is falling apart today, however.

For instance, Great Britain is actually made up of Scotland, England, Wales, and Northern Ireland. Historically, England conquered these other lands, and forced them to be part of England. Biblically speaking, however, England has no right to dominate Wales and Scotland. In recent years, the Welsh people have become insistent that their own language be used inside Wales. They have seen the language and culture of Cornwall (another nation subjugated by the English) completely disappear, and they do not want the same thing to happen to Welsh culture. Road signs in Wales must now have the Welsh words on top and the English underneath. And of course, some people in Wales want to separate from England altogether.

From time to time we hear of fire-bombings and other revolutionary actions perpetrated in Spain by the Basque or Catalonian nationalists. These nations have never wanted to be part of Spain and indeed were independent for a brief period during the Civil War of the 1930s. They just don't want their traditions swamped by Spanish culture. And why should they? While violent revolution is not the biblical way to obtain independence, we do need to ask by what right Spain imposes its government on these other cultures?

In France and Belgium, the Flemish are on the rise. A friend of mine, studying organ under the Flemish master Flor Peeters, told me of a difficulty he encountered. My friend did not know Flemish, so his lessons had to be conducted in another language. Both men spoke French fluently, but Flemish nationalist Peeters refused to use French. Thus, the lessons were conducted awkwardly in English, of which Peeters knew very little.

There is no particular reason why Bosnia, Herzegovina, Montenegro, Serbia, Croatia, Dalmatia, and Slovenia all have to be under one government (Yugoslavia). If they want to be, fine; if not, that's fine, too. And is there any reason why the Provencal-speaking Occitanians located in South France should be forced to remain under Parisian government if they don't want to be?

Of course, it is entirely possible for national*ism* to become idolatrous in character. The violence that has characterized some nationalistic movements points to this. All the same, such an idolatrous nationalism is a perversion that points to the truth of national integrity.

American foreign policy has shown itself committed to secularism rather than to Christianity when it comes to allowing freedom for the true nations. Two stories from African history will illustrate the point, but first some background.

When European countries divided up Africa among themselves, they did not bother with tribal (national) divisions and territories. They just drew lines on maps and enforced them. When these colonies became independent during the two decades after World War II, the European boundary lines continued to be in force. This has led to one grotesque horror after another in Africa. Some African nations were split between two states. In other cases, a dominant nation (tribe) acted to crush, or even exterminate, the other nations within the country.

The first horror story involving the United States is that of the former Belgian Congo, today known as Zaire. On June 30, 1960, the Congo was granted independence from Belgium. The new Prime Minister, Patrice Lumumba, took advantage of the independence ceremonies to launch a rabble-rousing attack on the continuing white presence in the Congo. This was particularly directed, it seems, against the nation of blacks living in Katanga province, for they were of a mind to cooperate with Europeans involved in their mining industry. A few days later, on July 5, the garrison in the capital city mutinied and also began to loot, rape, and kill both Europeans and Africans of other tribes. As the situation grew worse, the Belgians sought to restore order. In a similar move, Christian statesman Moise Tshombe separated his Katanga province from the rest of the country on July 13, declaring independence.

As we have noted, from a Christian point of view, there was no reason why the black nation of Katanga should have remained part of the meaningless agglomeration of peoples formerly called the Belgian Congo. But, from a secular humanist point of view, this separation was regarded as very, very bad indeed. The Secretary-General of the United Nations, Dag Hammarskjold, organized an army to force Katanga back into the Congo. Christian commentator Paul Johnson brilliantly pinpoints the character of this humanist hero: "In this forlorn endeavor, Hammarskjold paid scant regard to the lives, black or white, he was risking. Cold, detached, consumed by an overwhelming ambition masquerading as an ideal, he thought in terms of a political abstraction, not human beings."[12] Unfortunately for him, Hammarskjold "made the error of leaving the abstract

---

12 Paul Johnson, *Modern Times: The World from the Twenties to the Eighties* (New York, N.Y.: Harper and Row, 1983), 516.

make-believe world of his offices and descending into the real world of the Congo basin. It cost him his life when his aircraft hit a tree near Ndola in September 1961."

Before his death, Hammarskjold had created his own little war in the Congo. Anxious to appear on the side of humanism and big government, the Kennedy administration threw heavy support behind the U.N. intervention. By January, 1963, Katanga had been overrun by the U.N., after great slaughter. Thus the people of Katanga were crushed, with the help of the United States of America.

In one of the ironies of history, trouble broke out in the Congo again in 1964, and Moise Tshombe had to be recalled from exile to restore order. The rule of Christian peace was short-lived, however, for in December 1965, Joseph Mobutu overthrew the government in a military coup. "Thereafter, Mobutu, now president, ruled with the support of Western interests, to the enrichment of many hundreds of friends, supporters, and relatives, and not least of himself: By the early 1980s he was reckoned to be a billionaire, perhaps the world's wealthiest man...."

The second story is of Biafra and Nigeria. The British colony of Nigeria embraced basically four nations: the Hausa and Fulani in the north, the Ibo in the east, and the Yoruba in the west. The Hausas became dominant after independence. The Hausas are Moslem while the Ibos are Christian, and after a time the Hausa majority began severe persecutions of the Christian Ibos. On May 30, 1967, the Ibos separated from Nigeria and formed the country of Biafra. Two years of horrible civil war ensued, with the

---

13 Ibid., 516.

14 Ibid., 517. In a commentary on the grotesque situation, Paul Johnson tells us (on 531) that later on "Joseph Mobutu banned Christian names and re-named himself Monutu Sese Seko Kuku Ngbendu Wa Za Banga, freely translated as 'the cock that leaves no hens alone.'"

United States and Britain supporting Nigeria. As a result, the Ibos were crushed and forced back into a meaningless political union with the rest of Nigeria.

Sometimes Christian principles prevail, however. The white government of the Republic of South Africa has permitted and encouraged the various black nations to form their own governments in localities called homelands. Several such national governments have been created. This is certainly a move in the right direction, though it has not alleviated the problems caused by the policy of apartheid in other parts of the country.

In many of these cases, communist terrorists have seized upon the legitimate nationalistic desires of these peoples in order to promote turmoil and violence. The failure of the Christian West to make a strong affirmation of national and local integrity has opened the door for revolution. While it is not the business of the United States to meddle in the affairs of other states or nations, our Christian sympathies should clearly be with local peoples who wish to be free of the cultural imperialism of other nations. We certainly have no business supporting such imperialism, as we did in the Congo and in Nigeria.

While Christians can and should sympathize with the aspirations of peoples and nations to be free from oppression, we should not be naive. Too often, those who become leaders of "national fronts" are simply ambitious thugs, who are manipulating the proper aspirations of local people in order to enrich themselves. The legitimate "right of national determination" is often used as a cloak by which new petty tyrants come to power.

CONCLUSION

Biblical civil government is locally-centered, but secular humanism tends to always seek the formation of a massive civil state, imposing cultural unity by force and destroying the integrity of local nations and traditions. At Pentecost, God caused the gospel to be heard in many different languages, thus affirming the integrity of each nation, tribe, and tongue. Biblically speaking, each nation has the duty and right to work out its own destiny, unmolested by its neighbors.

Global Unity

I am not asking on behalf of these alone, but also for those who believe in Me through their word, that they may all be one; just as You, Father, are in Me and I in You, that they also may be in Us, so that the world may believe that You sent Me. The glory which You have given Me I also have given to them, so that they may be one, just as We are one.
— John 17:20-22 (New American Standard Bible)

The Bible and the Christian faith teach that God is Three, but He is also One. As the image of God, humanity was created one in Adam, and redeemed humanity is one in Christ. There is, thus, a legitimate principle of unity or oneness in human affairs, and the Christian faith is concerned to promote true unity in international affairs. What that means is the topic of our reflections in this chapter.

God definitely desires for humanity to form a "one-world order." The Bible shows this over and over. This one-world order is not based on might or power, but on the Spirit of God (Zech. 4:6). The Christian idea of a one-world order is not statist, but spiritual. Christopher Dawson describes this unity for us:

> For a thousand years Christian Europe has existed as a true supernatural society—a society that was intensely

> conscious of its community of culture in spite of the continual wars and internal divisions that made up its history. . . . Today this is no longer so. Europe has lost her unity and the consciousness of the spiritual mission. There is no longer any clear line of division between Christian and non-Christian peoples, and with the disappearance of her Christian consciousness, Europe has begun to doubt her own existence.[15]

What Dawson means is that in a Christian world there are many nations, many cultures, many languages, and many governments—but all share a common bond of faith and cooperation.

There is a true unity, not a unity at the level of the state, but a unity in the Church and in the faith. The Middle Ages, in spite of its problems, had such a unity.[16] That unity continued down to the modern era, but with the rise of neo-paganism (secular humanism),[17] that unity is being shattered, for as we saw in our first chapter, God will not permit pagans to unite.

THE BIBLICAL SYMBOL OF UNITY

When God created the world, He established many distinct lands. Humanity was put in the land of Eden, but there were rivers that flowed out of Eden to other lands, such as Havilah and Cush. As men multiplied and spread, they would move to these other lands and form new nations. While this gives us a picture of diversity, it also gives us a picture of unity.

---

15 Christopher Dawson, *The Judgment of the Nations* (New York, N.Y.: Sheed and Ward, 1942), 73.

16 T.S. Eliot, *Christianity and Culture*, "Notes Toward a Definition of Culture," (New York, N.Y.: Harcourt, Brace, and World, 1949). The unity and diversity of Christian European culture is the theme of T. S. Eliot's valuable study, "Notes Toward a Definition of Culture."

17 Peter Gay, *The Enlightenment: An Interpretation: The Rise of Modern Paganism* (New York, N.Y.: Knopf, 1966).

Gen. 2:10 says, "Now a river flowed out of Eden to water the garden; and from there it divided and became four rivers" (NASB). The following verses describe how these rivers spread out to the "four corners of the earth" in order to water all the lands. What we want to see here is that the water flowing from Eden to the whole world is the basic symbol of international unity.

Throughout the Bible, water is a symbol of life, because people cannot live without it (see for instance, Psalm 1:3; Exod. 15:22-27; 17:1-7; Num. 20:2-13; John 4:1-15; 7:38-39; Rev. 22:1). This life-giving water arises in the center of the world and flows out, bringing life to all lands. We see a picture of this in Ezekiel 47. Before we read that passage, we need to get some background.

The Bible is written very often in pictures, in terms of visual associations and parallels. We modern people don't tend to think in Bible pictures, but if we are going to understand the Bible, we shall have to learn to. Relevant to our study is one of the Bible's most fundamental pictures: the sanctuary and its waters.

During the Old Covenant, from Adam's sin to Jesus' resurrection, men were not permitted to rest in God's sanctuary.[18] They could bring their sacrifices to the gate of the sanctuary, but they could not go in. God would not permit His holy place to be defiled by sinful men. Cherubim stood at the gate to kill anyone who tried (Lev. 10:1-2). Just as these mighty angels stood at the gate of Eden to keep Adam and Eve out (Gen. 3:24), so they also stood at the gates of the Tabernacle and Temple later on:

---

18 James B. Jordan, Sabbath Breaking and the Death Penalty: A Theological Investigation (Tyler, Tex.: Geneva Ministries, 1986). After the Tabernacle was set up, the high priest was allowed to go in, but only for a few minutes once a year. He was not permitted to remain and rest. On this exclusion from Sabbath rest in the Old Covenant, see my book, Sabbath Breaking and the Death Penalty.

- They guarded the mercy seat (Exod. 25:18-22; 37:7-9; 1 Kings 6:23-28).
- They guarded the door to the Holy of Holies (Exodus 26:31-33; 36:35-36; 1 Kings 6:31-35).
- They guarded the whole perimeter of the Tabernacle and Temple (Exod. 26:1-6; 36:8-13; 1 Kings 6:29-30).
- They guarded God's portable Chariot-Throne (Ezek. 10).[19]

When we look at the Tabernacle and Temple, we find that each had a container of water. There was the "laver of cleansing" in the Tabernacle, and the "bronze ocean" in the Temple; but because of sin, none of this cleansing water ever flowed out to transform the world. Thus, as we shall see, during most of the Old Covenant the gospel did not really go out to the nations. Instead, the nations were brought to the central sanctuary—or to its gate, since they could not go in.

Not until the death of Jesus Christ were men permitted to go into God's sanctuary. The Book of Hebrews tells us one of the major purposes of the sacrificial system in the Old Covenant: "The Holy Spirit is signifying this, that the way into the holy place has not yet been disclosed while the outer tabernacle is still standing" (Heb. 9:8, NASB). So, once Jesus had opened heaven for us and had brought His people into possession of the New Covenant, God destroyed the Temple in Jerusalem because it was no longer needed.

Now, in the New Covenant, the river flows out once again. Spiritual life and power are no longer locked up in a closed sanctuary. This is pictured for us in the prophecy of Ezekiel 47, to which we can now turn our attention.[20]

---

19 Their presence was indicated by artistic symbolism: cherubim embroidered on the curtains.

20 Ezekiel's Temple symbolizes the spiritual state of affairs after the Jews

Ezekiel is being given a guided tour of a visionary Temple:

> Then he [the angelic guide] brought me [Ezekiel] back to the door of the house; and behold, water was flowing from under the threshold of the house toward the east, for the house faced east. And the water was flowing down from under, from the right side of the house, from south of the altar. (Ezek. 47:1, NASB)

Now, the right side of the temple, south of the altar, was where the "Sea of cast metal" was located (1 Kings 7:39). What has happened? God has tipped over this container of water, and cleansing water is flowing out of the temple.

Ezekiel goes out of the temple area and watches the water flow out. The angel starts to measure it:

> When the man went out toward the east with a line in his hand, he measured a thousand cubits, and he led me through the water, water reaching the ankles. Again he measured a thousand and led me through the water, water reaching the knees. Again he measured a thousand and led me through the water, water reaching the hips. Again he measured a thousand; and it was a river that I could not wade across, because the water had risen, enough water to swim in, a river that could not be crossed by wading. (Ezek. 47:3-5, NASB)

The water of life is flowing deeper all the way.

Now, we have been told that this water is flowing east from Jerusalem. A glance at a map will show that this is the area of the Dead Sea, of Sodom and Gomorrah. So

---

returned from exile, but it also points toward the New Covenant. After the exile, the Jews did carry the truth outward to the world, establishing synagogues in many lands.

Ezekiel's vision, however, limits the outflow of spiritual water to the land of Canaan itself. It remains for Revelations 22 to show the water going to all the world. Ezekiel's vision shows the principle of spiritual outflow operating in the centuries just before Christ, and that principle is still at work today in much greater force after the outpouring of the Spirit at Pentecost.

powerful are the gracious influences of this water that it will utterly transform the most wicked of all nations. The angel explains to Ezekiel, and to us:

> And he said to me, "Son of man, have you seen this?" Then he brought me [a]back to the bank of the river. 7 Now when I had returned, behold, on the bank of the river there were very many trees on the one side and on the other. 8 Then he said to me, "These waters go out toward the eastern region and go down into the Arabah; then they go toward the [b]sea, being made to flow into the sea, and the waters of the sea become [c]fresh. 9 And it will come about that every living creature which swarms in every place where the [d]river goes, will live. And there will be very many fish, for these waters go there and the others [e]become fresh; so everything will live where the river goes." (Ezek. 47:6-9, NASB)

The cleansing waters restore life to the land. The Garden of Eden is spiritually restored, and its waters once again go out to transform the nations. The angel tells Ezekiel one more thing that we need to notice:

> "And by the river on its bank, on one side and on the other, will grow all kinds of trees for food. Their leaves will not wither and their fruit will not fail. They will bear fruit every month because their water flows from the sanctuary, and their fruit will be for food and their leaves for healing." (Ezek. 47:12, NASB)

This is a picture of the kingdom of God, created by the Holy Spirit. The water pictures the outpouring of the Spirit, and the trees that grow in every place indicate the churches. The fruit of the trees represents the spiritual nourishment given by the Church to the world. The leaves represent the healing work of the Church in the world.

There are many nations, but one Church. There is only one kind of fruit: the fruit of the true Tree of Life, the body and blood of Jesus Christ. The true principle of unity is not found in some political union of nations but in the worldwide work of the Spirit and the Bride.

This same picture is found in Rev. 22:1-2, where it explicitly mentions the healing of the *nations*:

> And he showed me a river of the water of life, clear as crystal, coming from the throne of God and of the Lamb, in the middle of its street. On either side of the river was the tree of life, bearing twelve kinds of fruit, yielding its fruit every month; and the leaves of the tree were for the healing of the nations. (NASB)[21]

We see it again: many nations, but only one kind of tree, fed by the water of the Spirit, who proceeds from the Father and the Son (Lamb).

The biblical symbol of international unity is twofold: the water of life and the tree of life. The water symbolizes the life-giving work of the Spirit, poured out on Pentecost. The tree symbolizes the healing and feeding/nurturing work of the Bride, the Church.

A RE-CREATED WORLD

When God called Abraham out of Ur, He promised to give him all the things that sinful men had tried to seize at the Tower of Babel. Remember, the call of Abraham in Genesis 12 comes right after the Tower of Babel in Genesis 11. There

---

[21] The vision of Ezekiel 47 only shows the water reaching to the borders of the promised land. In redemptive historical context, this is a prophecy of the renewal of God's people after the exile. Thus, strictly speaking, it is only the healing of the promised land—the Jews—that is envisioned here. The prophecy of Ezekiel is, however, typologically related to the fullness of the New Covenant after Pentecost. The principles embodied in the vision of Ezekiel 47 find their greater realization in Revelations 22, which shows healing waters flowing in four directions, not just one, and to the whole world.

is a deliberate contrast. God says to Abraham, "And I will make you into a great nation, and I will bless you, and make your name great" (Gen. 12:2, NASB). Recall how Nimrod's people had said, "Let's make a name for ourselves" (Gen. 11:4, NASB); here God promises to make Abraham's name great. Finally, God says, "And in you all the families of the earth will be blessed" (Gen. 12:3, NASB).

This is the beginning of the ministry of the chosen people. They will serve all the other nations as priests. God will give them the sanctuary and the water, though only in certain limited ways, so that they can minister to all the other nations. A fine picture of Israel's calling to give water to the nations is seen in Gen. 26:12-33, where Isaac digs one well after another for the Philistines, who eventually bind themselves to him by covenant and become believers.

God established His true "Tower" of worship with Israel. This is pictured for us in Gen. 28:10-17. Jacob was fleeing from Esau:

> And he happened upon a particular place and spent the night there, because the sun had set; and he took one of the stones of the place and made it a support for his head, and lay down in that place. And he had a dream, and behold, a ladder was set up on the earth with its top reaching to heaven; and behold, the angels of God were ascending and descending on it. (Gen. 28:11-12, NASB)

This is just like the Tower of Babel, except that this ladder to heaven was set up through God's grace, not by man's defiant works. What does Jacob say when he awakes? "How awesome is this place! This is none other than the house of God, and this is the gate of heaven!" (Gen. 28:17, NASB). The word *Babel* means "gate of heaven." Babylon is the counterfeit; the Church is the true gate of heaven.

As we have seen, the Holy Spirit was not poured out in the Old Covenant. Throughout most of the Old Covenant period, this was signified by the water closed up in the tabernacle and temple. Instead of sending Israelites out as missionaries, God brought the nations to them. A look at a map will make this clear. Every caravan traveling between Africa to Asia had to go through the holy land. Every caravan traveling between Europe to Africa had to go through the holy land. And, because of the Caucasus Mountains, every caravan traveling between Europe and Asia would dip down through the borders of the holy land. This is why there is so much in the Bible about the "strangers in the land." There were always strangers passing through.

From all of this, we can see how God established Israel as a nation of priests in the center of the world for the purpose of bringing true Spiritual unity to all nations. The Church is now that "nation of priests," and she has the same task, except that now she is sent out with life-giving water to all lands.[22]

In the Old Covenant, the international unity of the world was seen in the one central temple in Jerusalem. All nations were tied to Jerusalem. Those who blessed the Jews were themselves blessed. Those who cursed them were cursed (Gen. 12:3). The Godly Gentiles who understood this always acted to build up Jerusalem, because they knew it was for their benefit (see Ezra 1 for an example).

In the New Covenant, there is no longer any central earthly sanctuary. Rather, the "gate of heaven" is found in every place that the Church is established. The Church ministers as the Tree of Life to heal the nations. And since the Church is the same everywhere, she is the embodiment of international unity. The only true "united nations" is the Church herself.

---

22 As we noted in footnote 23 above, this outflow was anticipated in a provisional way by the international missions of the Jews in the centuries immediately preceding Christ.

A UNITED CHURCH

Is the Church really united? Is there only one international Church? It does not seem so when we look around. We see many denominations, many factions. How can we call this situation united?

And so it may appear to the eye of doubt. The Bible tells us clearly, however, that the Church is always perfectly united, despite appearances. If the Church does not *act* united, that is a problem; but whether she herself realizes it or not, the Church is always perfectly united.

How do we know this? Because Jesus asked the Father to keep the Church united, and the Father never denies the Son anything. Jesus prayed:

> I am not asking on behalf of these alone, but also for those who believe in Me through their word, that they may all be one; just as You, Father, are in Me and I in You, that they also may be in Us, so that the world may believe that You sent Me. The glory which You have given Me I also have given to them, so that they may be one, just as We are one; I in them and You in Me, that they may be perfected in unity, so that the world may know that You sent Me, and You loved them, just as You loved Me. (John 17:20-23, NASB)

Some may say, that's strictly an *invisible* unity. Not so. The Bible says that, despite what men think, there is "one Lord, one faith, *one baptism*" (Eph. 4:5). Baptism is visible. In fact, baptism is that water we've been talking about. The water of baptism is what makes us grow into Trees of Life, with leaves to heal our nations.

There is also one *visible (audible) Word of God*: the Bible. There may be many translations, but there is only one Bible. You can see it anywhere. And, there is *visibility* (tangibility) in the sacrament of holy communion. There is *only one bread and only one cup*, because there is only one Christ on whom we feed in the Spirit.

So the Church is always united. It is a sad thing that Christians so often don't act in terms of this, but the Church is indeed united, whether they realize it or not.

On Sunday morning when we draw into God's throne room to render Him formal obeisance, we are all in the same heavenly chamber. We may not see our Chinese and Ukrainian brethren any more than we see the angels and "the spirits of the righteous made perfect" in our midst, but they are all there with us in the same most holy place (Heb. 12:22-26, NASB). This is international unity in the purest and fullest sense. This is international brotherhood. This is the foundation for all other forms of international unity and cooperation.

THE NURSERY OF THE KINGDOM

The Church is the nursery of the Kingdom. All the principles that we have to use in our wider life, in state, school, business, and family, are found in the Church. The Church has a government like the state. She is a family for believers. Her husbandry of the tithe is in some ways analogous to the economics of a business enterprise. In all these ways, the Church serves as a new community in the earth, a training ground for the transformation of each nation and people.

The story of the Tower of Babel tells us that paganism (secular humanism) cannot provide a common culture for the nations. The Christian faith, acting as a nursery for the nations, does provide such a common culture. Each nation will be different, but each nation will be Christian and united in the common faith.

Thus, Christianity transforms the nations from the inside out, from the bottom up, from the nursery of the Church to the fullness of all Kingdom activities. The quiet, life-changing ministry of the Church works to create true unity among all peoples.

Secular humanism works in exactly the opposite manner. For pagans, unity is something imposed from above by the power and force of the state (the conqueror). For the humanist, unity comes about when several states (rulers) form alliances without regard to truth. Such secular unity has no inner principle holding it together. It is simply held together by force and convenience. As we see in the next essay in this series, the secular humanist scheme actually makes international relations impossible. Every attempt to build a Tower of Babel results in the scattering of those involved.

The Church and the faith can create a one world order. A picture of this is seen in Jesus' Parable of the Mustard Seed:

> The kingdom of heaven is like a mustard seed, which a person took and sowed in his field; and this is smaller than all the other seeds, but when it is fully grown, it is larger than the garden plants and becomes a tree, so that the birds of the sky come and nest in its branches. (Matt. 13:31b-32, NASB)

We have seen that the tree is usually a symbol for the people of God, the Church. That is clearly the case here, since it is the "kingdom of heaven" that is said to be like the tree. What does Jesus mean by the "birds of the sky," however? The explanation for this is given in the Old Testament. The pagan nations were often depicted as birds. There is a parable in Ezekiel 17, the Parable of the Cedar Tree, that resembles Jesus' parable:

> This is what the Lord God says: "I will also take a sprig from the lofty top of the cedar and set it out; I will break off from the topmost of its young twigs a tender one, and I will plant it on a high and lofty mountain. On the high

> mountain of Israel I will plant it, so that it may bring forth branches and bear fruit, and become a stately cedar. And birds of every kind will nest under it; they will nest in the shade of its branches." (Ezek. 17:22-23, NASB)

There is *one tree*, ministering to *birds of every kind*. The branches of the tree support the birds; the fruit of the tree feeds the birds; the shade of the tree protects the birds. So it is with the Church and the nations. The Church supports, feeds, and protects the nations.

God's foreign policy? World missions. How remarkable it is to go into a small, faithful church in a country town and find prominently displayed a world map. Pins on the map mark missionaries supported by the tiny church. Thus even the humblest of Christians have a true global vision. Quietly and without fanfare, the Church labors internationally to transform the world.

The more successful this foreign policy becomes, the more the world will be at true unity, and at peace. But apart from the missionary thrust of Christianity, there will be no unity, and no peace.

CONCLUSION

While secular humanism generally thinks of the oneness of humanity in statist terms, the Christian sees true unity as possible only in Christ. The original unity of humanity was shattered by Adam's sin, but it can be restored when men turn to the Second Adam, Jesus Christ. Not all men repent, however, so that total unity among all men is impossible. Not until the wicked are removed from the presence of the righteous can there be full unity. All the same, the more successful the mission of the Church becomes, the more men and nations will find ways to express their unity in Christ.

International Relations

So Hiram gave Solomon all that he wished of the cedar and juniper timber. Solomon then gave Hiram twenty thousand kors of wheat as food for his household, and twenty kors of pure oil; this is what Solomon would give Hiram year by year.

— 1 Kings 5:10-11 (New American Standard Bible)

God is Three and One. The three Persons of God do not exist in isolation from one another. Rather, they exist in covenant alliance. They exist in relationships. The Bible teaches us that the Father begets the Son, and the Son is the only-begotten of the Father (John 1:14, 18). The Spirit proceeds from the Father and the Son (John 15:26), though not in the same way, since the Father and Son are different Persons.[23]

---

23 For theological readers: (1) The Spirit proceeds from the Father. Since the Son is the image of the Father, (2) the Spirit also proceeds from the Son. Since the Son is a unique person, different from the Father, the procession of the Spirit from the Son differs from His procession from the Father. In addition to proceeding from the Father and also from the Son, (3) the Spirit proceeds from the Father and the Son together. Finally, since the Son is the Son of the Father, (4) the Spirit proceeds

Moreover, the three Persons cooperate in all that they do. In creating the world, the Father planned, the Son administered, and the Spirit executed the work of the plan. In redemption, the Father sent the Son to bear our sins, the Son worked out our salvation, and the Spirit applies it to us. These are cooperative projects based on the *relationships* the three Persons of God have between and among themselves.

As we have noted before, humanity is created to image God. People are supposed to cooperate with each other and form alliances. Marriage is one such "covenantal alliance." Business partnerships are another. There are all kinds of complex relationships that people sustain one with one another.

The same is ideally true of nations. Had man not fallen, there would be no reason why nations would avoid cooperating with each other in many kinds of ways. Cultural isolationism is un-Scriptural. The Son is not "isolated" from the Spirit, and neither should one nation be "isolated" from any others.

For the secularist, unfortunately, everything is political. He thinks only in terms of the Tower of Babel, political union based ultimately on force. We take up the subject of political alliances between nations later in these chapters (Chapter 6), but for now we concern ourselves with the more important and fundamental kinds of international relations. Foundationally, we shall have to look at *trade*.

THE DISTRIBUTION OF RESOURCES

Once again, our key passage is from Genesis 2. Here we have the river that flows to the four lands. We are told some interesting details about the land of Havilah: "The name

---

from the Father through the Son. Each of these four relationships must be allowed to stand without being absorbed into each other. There is mystery here, and we must avoid any kind of rationalistic reductionism.

of the first is Pishon; it flows around the whole land of Havilah, where there is gold. The gold of that land is good; the bdellium and the onyx stone are there as well" (Gen. 2:11-12). This information might seem pretty irrelevant to the creation account of Genesis 1 and 2, but like every detail in the Bible, it is included for an important reason.

These verses point to the distribution of resources. They imply that gold was not found in Eden. Adam would have to go downstream to Havilah to get it. We know from later scriptures that God wanted His sanctuary to be adorned with gold. (Read the descriptions of the Tabernacle and Temple in Exodus 25-40 and 1 Kings 5-7.) For this to take place, there would have to be trade between Eden and Havilah.

Of course, Adam fell and was kicked out of the Garden/sanctuary. The principle stayed in force, however. Men would have to engage in trade, for no single nation would be given enough resources to be totally independent.

Men did not want to move out and take dominion, however. They tried to stay in one place. At the Tower of Babel, God forced them out. He forced them to diversify. As we have seen, God did two fundamental things at the Tower of Babel. He divided their ideologies, so that sinful man would never be able to unify and attain to the power that comes from true unity. Second, He divided their actual languages, so that they would be forced to move away from each other and form new nations.

There is evidence to suggest that the Tower of Babel was part of a larger Divine program to diversify humanity and create the conditions needed for trade and cooperation, even by altering the earth itself. For example, many Bible-believing scientists suggest that before the Flood, the whole earth shared basically the same climate. They point to such things as the mammoths found frozen in Siberia with tropical plants in their mouths. After the Flood the climate over the earth seems to have become much more diversified, doubtless bringing with it a greater diversification of plant and animal life.

Another diversification may have been continental drift. Some Christian thinkers believe that this is pointed to in Gen. 10:25, which reads, "Two sons were born to Eber; the name of the one was Peleg, for in his days the earth was divided; and his brother's name was Joktan." This verse may refer to the Tower of Babel, but Nimrod was the third generation from Ham, while Peleg was the fifth generation from Shem. It is more likely that the Tower of Babel happened about fifty years before Peleg. In that case, this verse could refer to continental drift.

The continental drift theory passes in and out of favor with geologists. Presently most geologists think that the continental drift theory is correct. If so, then we can suggest the following: At creation and during the Flood, God scattered resources unevenly. After the Flood, God established the conditions that would make for a much greater diversity of climate in the world. After a couple of generations, God scattered humanity from the Tower of Babel. Men began to move away from one another. And possibly, about fifty years later God caused the continents to pull apart, carrying various portions of humanity with them.

What is the positive effect of these events? Just this: It makes trade necessary. No one geographical area is sufficient unto itself, so men need to learn cooperation. They have to learn to help one another through trade and bartering.

Moreover, the division of humanity into various races implies that different nations have skills in different areas. Some are better craftsmen, some better musicians, and so forth. (Remember, we are speaking of relatively small nations, not whole races of people.) An exchange of skills is necessary for any real cultural development and progress.

FOREIGNERS AND FREE TRADE

Because trade is so important to international relations, it is important that trade be free of civil laws that restrict voluntary trade, except in wartime. In this section, we want to look at the principle of free trade.

In pagan thought, the foreigner is always viewed with suspicion as an alien, an outsider, a "barbarian." In the ancient world, foreigners were often regarded as sub-human, and even until recent years some racist groups have maintained that the black nations are sub-human.

This viewpoint is, of course, thoroughly anti-Christian. All men descend from Adam, so all are equally human. Moreover, the Bible insists that foreigners be given equal protection under the law. Exod. 12:49 says, "The same law shall apply to the native as to the stranger who resides among you" (NASB; see also Lev. 24:22). Laws protecting the stranger and guaranteeing him equal justice include Exod. 20:10; 22:21; 23:9; Lev. 19:32-34 ("You shall love him as yourself"); Deut. 10:19; 14:29; 23:7; 24:14-22; 26:11-13. The kindness that Israel was required to show to strangers was, as we saw in Chapter 3, part of her missionary task; but it was also a simple reflection of the fundamental humaneness of the true religion.

Now, to see the economic implications of these laws we need to remind ourselves of who these strangers were. They were not aliens who had settled in the land. When Israel was given the land, it was parceled out in family lots. These lots always reverted to the original families in the Year of Jubilee, every fifty years (Leviticus 25). Thus, no foreigner could ever permanently possess land in

Israel. They could live in the cities, but never hold land outside. Gentile converts could travel to the holy land to take part in the Feast of Tabernacles, which particularly celebrated the conversion of the seventy nations (Gen. 10; Num. 29:12-34—seventy bulls for seventy nations; Hag. 2:1, 7; Zech. 14:16), but then they had to go back to their own nations. Such was the evangelistic strategy. Only if the foreigner became circumcised and joined one of the tribes, thus becoming part of Israel, could he become a landholder—but then he was no longer a Gentile convert but a Jew, one of the priestly nation. (This is as good a point as any to note that God generously saved many Gentiles during the Old Testament. We discuss this in more detail in Chapter 6.)

So who were these strangers in the land that the Bible keeps referring to, if they were not aliens who had settled there? They were caravaners and traders. There were to be no economic sanctions against foreign traders. The laws we have mentioned above make this clear, but there is one law in particular that spells it out: "You shall not have in your bag differing weights, a large and a small" (Deut. 25:13, NASB). Most financial transactions were conducted by weight of gold and silver pieces, and this law thus forbids any type of double standard, whether private cheating or legalized discrimination against foreigners.

Now you can imagine what could happen. Jacob ben Aaron is a shoemaker. He has been doing good business, selling shoes at about three copper shekels a pair. Then a caravan of strangers comes to town. They have good shoes that they are selling for two shekels each. Jacob ben Aaron is upset. "Buy Israelite," he cries. He goes to the elders of the town. He wants them to put a tariff on these foreign goods, a tax that will force them to raise their price to 3.2 shekels a pair. This will protect his business, thinks Jacob ben Aaron. But the law forbids it. The elders say, "Sorry, Jacob, but you will have to compete. The market is open to all, even 'dirty foreigners.' Either drop your prices, get out of the shoe business, or strike up a deal with the caravaners and purchase their shoe concession. You can buy their shoes at wholesale and sell them at retail; then you stay in business, and everyone is happy. But we won't let you oppress these foreigners."

In our modern world, tariff laws are the way the "have" nations, such as the United States, discriminate against the "have not" nations. People in poorer nations are willing to work for less and produce quality goods more cheaply. We protect one segment of our industry by putting high import taxes on these goods. This policy is grossly oppressive and anti-Christian. It reinforces and even creates negative feelings toward foreigners, and reflects a pagan mindset. Moreover, it penalizes our exports because foreigners are not earning our money to spend on our goods. We return to the subject of free trade in Chapter 13. For now, our point is that the relationships between nations and peoples are usually to be totally open in the area of trade.

INTERNATIONAL RELATIONS

While the people of Israel were not to seek out political and military alliances with other nations, they were free to trade with them. Isaac went to Egypt for grain during the famine, and Solomon procured from Hiram of Tyre the cedars of Lebanon to build the Temple. Such free trade opened opportunities for cross-cultural exchanges that benefited everyone.

The pagan mindset, with its fear of foreigners and its opposition to free trade, works against international relations. For instance, American and European relationships with the Japanese are vexed continually because of their intricate informal barriers to trade and the formal barriers erected by the United States and European nations. Such economic oppression frequently lead to war, as when the Southern States seceded from the Union because of Lincoln's tariffs, which crippled Southern farming. It is often said that where goods do not cross borders, armies will. This may not be true in every case, but it is a proverb with much wisdom in it all the same.

When we as Christians think of international relations and foreign policy, high on our agenda must be a return to the true fraternity of free trade. It is an essential element in God's foreign policy.

THE DEVELOPMENT OF TRUE INTERNATIONAL RELATIONS

Free trade is fine as far as it goes, and it does make for peace among nations. The interweaving of the nations in the plan of God, however, goes far deeper than the mere barter of goods. We can get a glimmer of the possibilities for a Christian world as we look at the history of European culture. T. S. Eliot, in his *Notes Toward the Definition of Culture*, wrestles with the nature of international unity and diversity within a Christian matrix. Summarizing his efforts, he writes:

> For the health of the culture of Europe two conditions are required: that the culture of each country should be unique [our principle of Integrity], and that the different cultures should recognize their relationship to each other, so that each should be susceptible of influence from the others [our principle of Relationships]. And this is possible because there is a common element in European culture, an interrelated history of thought and feeling and behaviour, an interchange of arts and of ideas [our principle of Unity].[24]

---

24 Eliot, *Christianity and Culture*, 197. Material in brackets added.

According to Eliot, the unity of Europe, which creates its common culture, is Christianity:

> I am talking about the common tradition of Christianity which has made Europe what it is, and about the common cultural elements which this common Christianity has brought with it. If Asia were converted to Christianity tomorrow, it would not thereby become a part of Europe. It is in Christianity that our arts have developed; it is in *Christianity* that the laws of Europe have—until recently—been rooted. It is against a background of Christianity that all our thought has significance...I do not believe that the culture of Europe could survive the complete disappearance of the Christian Faith. And I am convinced of that, not merely because I am a Christian myself, but as a student of social biology. If Christianity goes, the whole of our culture goes. Then you must start painfully again, and you cannot put on a new culture ready made. You must wait for the grass to grow to feed the sheep to give the wool out of which your new coat will be made. You must pass through many centuries of barbarism.[25]

True international relations, says Eliot, have little to do with politics. Furthermore:

> What I wish to say is, that this unity in the common elements of culture, throughout many centuries, is the true bond between us. No political and economic organisation, however much goodwill it commands, can supply what this culture unity gives. It we dissipate or throw away our common patrimony of culture [that is, Christian culture as developed in Europe], then all the organisation and planning of the most ingenious minds will not help us, or bring us closer together.[26]

---

25 Ibid., 200.

26 Ibid., 201.

CONCLUSION

The purpose of this essay has been to set forth the positive side of international relations. Considered as cultures, nations should have relationships primarily through trade. While we have focused on the economic side of trade—"free trade"—there is also the interchange of ideas and arts. Such exchanges are particularly important among Christian nations.

At this point, it will be useful to summarize the Christian philosophy we have been developing. In the preceding three chapters, we have set out the three fundamental principles of international relations. Humanity was made to image the life of God. God is Three and One, and humanity is both unified and diverse.

In Chapter 2, we saw that the three-ness of God implies the integrity of each nation. That integrity is not to be violated. The heart of the pagan one-world scheme is to violate that integrity and create a monolithic, non-diverse culture.

In Chapter 3, we saw that the oneness of God implies the development of a *Godly* one-world order. That one-world order comes to expression first of all in the Church, which is always one in Christ. By extension, the Christian faith works to create oneness and cooperation among peoples of all nations. The heart of the pagan scheme is to ignore differences of faith and create a *political* one-world state. This is the age-old imperial dream, whether ancient Assyrian or modern Secular Humanist.

In Chapter 4, we saw that the interrelationships among the Persons of God imply international relations. The heart of such relations is free trade, both of goods and of arts and ideas. The pagan scheme works to destroy free trade by means of tariffs and import taxes, thus setting the stage for wars of economic aggression.

At every point, the Christian viewpoint is the reverse of the pagan. A chart[27] will help set this out:

Christian unity:		Pagan unity:
One worldwide faith		*One world state*
Christian cooperation	vs.	Pagan (non-)cooperation:
Free trade	vs.	*Tariffs*
Arts & Ideas	vs.	*Suspicion & Hostility*
Christian diversity:		Pagan diversity:
Many nations and governments		*Many religions*

Notice the diagonal lines. First, notice that the pagan unity of a one-world state (actually a one-state world) is diametrically opposed to the Christian diversity of many nations and local governments. At the same time, notice that the Christian unity of one worldwide faith (Christianity) is diametrically opposed to the pagan diversity of many religions.

Notice, second, that the Christian system is mutually reinforcing. The one faith of Christianity works to reinforce the integrity of local county-sized government and national integrity, and vice versa.

Finally, notice that the pagan system is mutually destructive. The multitude of diverse religions established at the Tower of Babel will always work to undermine the pagan dream of a one-world state, and the one-world state will work to crush the diversity of religions.

---

27 This kind of diagram is called "Frame's square," after Professor John M. Frame, who developed it.

What we see from this is that *eventually only the Christian system will work*. The pagan, secular humanist dream cannot work. It never has, and it never will. It leads to war and death. The Christian system will work. It has in the past, and it will in the future.

From here we go to several secondary principles, implications of our Trinitarian model, that are important for us to consider as we reflect on international relations. In Chapter 5, we investigate the subject of *boundaries* and the right to protect boundaries by means of military might. In Chapter 6, we take up the question of political and military *alliances* between Christian nations. In Chapter 7, we apply the principles of Chapter 6 to United States foreign policy. In Chapter 8, we look at the principle of *presence* and the need for communication among all nations. In Chapter 9, we apply these principles to a critique of the secular humanist United Nations. In Chapter 10, we consider the principle of *sanctuary* and its relevance for discipling the nations. In Chapter 11, we apply these sanctuary principles to the problem of immigration today. Finally, in Chapter 12, we summarize what a Christian foreign policy should look like.

National Boundaries

As the mountains surround Jerusalem, so the Lord surrounds His people from this time and forever.
— Psalm 125:2 (New American Standard Bible)

The integrity of the nations is derived, as we have seen, from their creation in the image of God, who is Three as well as One. Each Person of the Trinity has His own integrity. This is imaged in humanity by the integrity of each individual person, of each family, of each local church and county, and of each nation. Such integrity implies boundaries.

Biblically speaking, the idea of integrity and boundaries is what is meant by "holiness." God is holy, which means He has integrity of character and a moral boundary around Himself, in terms of what He permits or does not permit to be near to Him. We are to be holy as He is holy, which means we are to have integrity of character in His image and likeness.

God has a boundary around Himself that is called His "glory." This glory appears in the Bible sometimes as a cloud, sometimes as a rainbow around His throne, sometimes as "holy ground" around Him, and so forth. As we have already seen, the cherubim guard this boundary, which was represented by the walls and curtains of the Temple and Tabernacle, as well as by the mountains surrounding Jerusalem (Psalm 125:2).

Similarly, each of us has a boundary around himself or herself. Sometimes people call this their "space." We don't like it if a stranger gets right up in our face and talks to us, or if he acts too chummy by putting his arm around us. This violates our "space." We only let certain people into our personal space.

The same is true of our families. You don't horn in on somebody else's family life. And, since property is generally owned by families, you don't violate someone else's property either.

In this way, the integrity of each unit is guarded by a boundary. The Bible is not silent on this subject. At the personal and family levels, the Bible guarantees the privilege of the private ownership and government of property (Exod. 20:15; Lev. 25:13; 1 Kings 21). At the county level, the Bible devotes seven chapters (Joshua 13-19) to setting out fixed governmental boundaries for the Israelite tribes.

At the national level, God also set boundaries for the nations. Paul said to the Athenians, "And He made from one man every nation of mankind to live on all the face of the earth, having determined their appointed times and the boundaries of their habitation" (Acts 17:26, NASB). Because national boundaries are fluid, as peoples move and change, Paul says that God appointed "times" as well as boundaries.

Accordingly, when Israel came out of Egypt, they asked permission of the king of Edom before crossing his boundary. Moses was most specific in his respect for the Edomite boundary:

> Please let us pass through your land. We will not pass

> through field or vineyard; we will not even drink water from a well. We will go along the king's road, not turning to the right or left, until we pass through your territory. (Num. 20:17, NASB)

The king of Edom said no, however, and Israel respected him and traveled by another route (Num. 20:18-21).

In this essay, we want to reflect on three implications of the Biblical concept of national boundary. The first is that each nation should pretty much mind its own business. The second is that every nation deserves "recognition." The third is that boundaries may be defended by military might.

MIND YOUR OWN BUSINESS

Christian nations do have "business" in common, and it is legitimate to form mutual defense pacts and other kinds of treaties to take care of this mutual business. For the most part, however, nations are to mind their own affairs, just as individuals and families do.

Prov. 26:17 says that "like one who takes a dog by the ears, so is one who passes by and meddles with strife not belonging to him" (NASB). The dog here is not a trained dog or a house pet, but one of the wild scavenger dogs that roamed the ancient world. Take him by the ears and be prepared to be seriously injured.

The American forefathers understood this principle. In his Farewell Address, George Washington admonished the people of the United States:

> Why, by interweaving our destiny with that in any part of Europe, entangle our peace and prosperity in the toils of European ambition, rivalship, interest, humor, or

> caprice...? 'Tis our true policy to steer clear of permanent alliance....Taking care to keep ourselves on a respectable defensive posture, we may safely trust to temporary alliances for extraordinary emergencies....[28]

This relative or partial "isolationism" kept the United States healthy for a long time, but around the turn of the 20th century, American foreign policy underwent a change. Theodore Roosevelt believed that Americans needed to take a role in international disputes. One of his actions brought about disastrous consequences.

The Russians and the Japanese got into a war over Manchuria, which ended in 1905 with a decisive Japanese victory.[29] Roosevelt allowed himself to be seduced into acting as an arbiter of peace. Roosevelt gave the Russians much more than Japan wanted him to, and the Japanese were angry. In the years that followed, ever more highly militaristic and imperialistic influences came to power in Japan. They did not forget the United States, as the world found out at Pearl Harbor.

Since the days of the Open Door Policy (originally restricted to China) of the late 1800s, the United States has greatly expanded its presence in the world. While there is a limited value in having embassies and consulates in other countries, there is no justification for the vast extent of the American presence worldwide. From a Christian standpoint, the American government should greatly

---

28 George Washington, "Founders Online: Farewell Address, 19 September 1796," National Archives and Records Administration, July 27, 2018. https://founders.archives.gov/documents/Washington/99-01-02-00963

29 This foolish endeavor also eventually cost the Tsar in the Russian Revolution. For one intelligent historian's scathing look at this unpopular war, take in Nicolai Rimski-Korsakoff's opera, *The Golden Cock*, which was completed in 1907. Performance of this opera was prohibited until after the Revolution.

reduce the number of people it maintains in foreign lands, for no good can come of it. We take up United States foreign policy in more detail in Chapter 7.[30]

RECOGNITION

For years, the secular humanist government of the United States has maintained a policy of "recognizing" some countries and not "recognizing" others. This policy is based on a set of humanist values and is designed to manipulate other governments. The most grotesque illustration of this in recent years has been the de-recognition of Free China (Taiwan) in favor of recognition of Communist China. This policy is absurd and unbiblical.

From a biblical standpoint, each nation is to mind its own business. To the extent that one nation needs to have dealings with another, it should simply do what is needful by granting "recognition" to whatever powers there may be.

The question comes up, of course, when a nation has a civil war or undergoes a radical change of government. Shall we "recognize" the new government? Two principles can help us assess the new government: (1) Does it pose a military threat to us? (2) Did it throw out a Christian government illegally?

But suppose the civil war concerned only internal matters? Whom do we "recognize?" That is a tricky question, and it is best simply to avoid the issue by not "recognizing" anyone and just dealing with whomever we have to deal with. In that way, we can deal both with "new puppet regimes" and with "true governments in exile."

---

[30] The non-American reader should bear in mind that the writer of these essays is a citizen of the United States, and that they were originally aimed at an American audience.

At the same time, there are two principles that help us in thinking about our involvement with other nations and countries. The first is that Christian thought places more value on peoples and nations than on states and governments. That is, in our thinking we "recognize" not simply the powers-that-be in our world, but also the peoples and nations. Until recently, for instance, the Azerbaijani and Ukrainian nations were enslaved to the Soviet state. If we must have dealings with an empire like the Soviet state, this should not cause us to forget the reality of these peoples. They deserve our sympathy in their sufferings and in their attempts to free themselves from the yoke of the oppressor.

The second principle is that there is a difference between Christian and non-Christian countries and nations. Part of our "business" is to stand with all Christian peoples against the enemies of Christ, and as we "mind our business" as a Christian nation, we shall naturally have more to do with other Christian nations than with pagan ones. We return to this in Chapter 6 when we discuss alliances. For now, the point is that there can clearly be greater cooperation between Christian nations and a place in them for larger embassies and consulates than there can be between Christian and pagan nations.

DEFENSE

Boundaries may and should be defended. The Bible establishes the right of self-defense in Exod. 22:2, which says that if a thief "is caught while breaking in and is struck so that he dies, there will be no guilt for bloodshed on his account" (NASB). The Bible provides six general principles of warfare that need to be taken into account.

The first is that *war must never be aggressive*. The rulers of Israel were forbidden to "multiply horses" (Deut. 17:16). What this means becomes clearer when we consider the nature of ancient warfare. Horses and chariots were used only in aggressive warfare. There was no need to maintain a large body of these for any other purpose. Defensive warfare meant good strong walls and a well-trained local militia. The integrity of each nation under God means that aggression and conquest are never permitted.

The second principle is *crushing the head*. The Bible holds the leaders of society primarily responsible for social decisions. Thus, the most important matter in victory over an invading army is the destruction of its leadership.

Assassination of the heads of the enemy state is a foremost biblical principle of war. This is seen particularly in the Book of Judges, where in each case it is the heads of state that are the primary target of the battle, for when the leader dies, the army scatters. Thus, Ehud assassinated Eglon (Judges 3); Jael killed Sisera (Judges 4, 5); Gideon slew Zebah, Zalmunna, Oreb, and Zeeb (Judg. 7:25; 8:21). When Saul sought to spare Agag, who was after all "fellow royalty," his sin was so great that it cost him the crown (1 Sam. 15:8-9, 20-33). The principle of assassinating the heads of aggressor states is just in that it punishes those who are responsible, but it is also simpler and less costly. (Of course, a leader who uses assassination as a tool of war increases the likelihood that others will use it against him, which is why modern nations have a "gentlemen's agreement" not to practice assassination. From a biblical standpoint, it requires a lot of faith in God's protection to employ the tool of assassination!)

The third principle is the *offer of peace*. This is seen in Deut. 20:10ff. The law states, "When you approach a city to fight against it, you shall offer it terms of peace" (NASB). Since Israel was to exterminate all the Canaanites (Deut. 20:15-18), this only applied to a city outside the land. Since only defensive wars were allowed, we must ask under what conditions Israel might become involved in fighting against a city far away. We have to assume that this city or nation had launched an attack against Israel. Defeated in battle, the invaders have been beaten back to the walls of their city. At this point, the offer of peace by Israel is credible, for she has already shown herself to be militarily superior on the battlefield. What we learn from this is that total war and unconditional surrender are not biblical military principles. The carrot of a negotiated peace is to be offered right up to the end.[31]

The fourth principle is that *the land is not to be wasted* in warfare (Deut. 20:19-20). What this means in principle is that war is to be made against warmongers, not against everything and everyone residing in the enemy nation. The law is phrased in terms of trees; fruit trees are not to be cut down and used in siege works. Since, however, trees are a standard symbol for men (Psalm 1, Judges 9), the law is intended to apply to living men as well as to trees. Civilians are not to be attacked. A policy of "mutually assured destruction" is not a Christian option.[32]

The fifth principle is *universal participation*. Every able-bodied man was to be ready to fight to preserve the nation (Judges 21; Deut. 20:1-9). A small company of crack troops might be maintained as a small professional army ready to take the brunt of an initial attack, but the main defense of the nation was the job of the citizen militia. Thus, each Israelite had the "right and duty to bear arms."[33]

---

[31] Russell Grenfell, *Unconditional Hatred: German War Guilt and the Future of Europe* (Old Greenwich, Conn.: Devin-Adair, 1953). On the evil effects of a policy of "unconditional surrender," especially as these came to light in World War II, see Grenfell's work.

[32] James B. Jordan, "Ecological Sin in a Difficult Passage (2 Kings 3)," *Biblical Horizons* 171 (July, 2004).

[33] James B. Jordan, The Militia in 20th Century America: A Symposium, "The Israelite Militia in the Old Testament," edited by Morgan Norval (Falls Church, Va.: Gun Owners Foundation, 1985). I have discussed this matter at length and given more information on biblical principles of

The sixth principle is *localism*. A study of the battles in Judges shows that those near the battle were expected to send more men and support the war more heavily than those farther away. Some token of support, however, was expected from every tribe. How much was expected also depended on the seriousness of the situation. At any rate, the principle is that local men defend their local situation.

BOUNDARIES, REVISITED

Now, this raises the question of boundaries once again. If a thief breaks into your home at night and you don't know whether or not he is going to kill you, you can go ahead and kill him first (Exodus 22:2). He has crossed the boundary of your home as an aggressor.

We are used to thinking of Israel as a nation with a boundary, fighting occasional defensive wars to protect that boundary. Actually, though, as we see in Chapter 6, Israel was in some ways a league of thirteen Christian tribal republics. Each had its own boundary to defend. We find references to particular tribes fighting wars and defending their own boundaries without calling in the whole nation.

There is an important principle embedded in this point, so permit me to quote from E. C. Wines at some length to summarize what the Bible says about it:

> The powers reserved to the separate tribes, and freely exercised by them, were very great. We find them often acting like independent nations. This was the case not only when there was neither king nor judge in the

---

war in my essay, "The Israelite Militia in the Old Testament." Also published in Larry Pratt, ed., Safeguarding Liberty: The Constitution and Civilian Militias (Franklin, Tenn.: Legacy Communications, 1995).
Jordan, Judges: God's War Against Humanism (Tyler, Tex.: Geneva Ministries, 1985), retitled Judges: A Practical and Theological Commentary (Eugene, Oreg.: Wipf and Stock, 1999). Extended discussions of biblical warfare can be found in my commentary on Judges.

> land, but even under the government of the kings. They levied war and made peace, whenever it seemed good to them. Thus we find Joshua exhorting his brethren, the children of Joseph, to make war against the Perizzites; and Zebulon and Naphtali uniting to fight against Jabin (Joshua 17:15; Judges 4:10). . . . A very remarkable record of this kind is contained in the fifth chapter of 1 Chronicles (1 Chronicles 5:18-23). It is there related that the tribes beyond the Jordan, even in the reign of Saul, carried on, upon their own responsibility, a most important war.... Four nations were leagued together against the trans-jordanic tribes in this war.... The entire territories of these nations came into the possession of the Hebrews as the fruit of this contest, "and they dwelt in their steads until the captivity." As late as the reign of Hezekiah, we see the tribe of Simeon waging two successful wars, one against the inhabitants of Gedor, and the other against the remnant of the Amalekites, and that without aid or authority from its neighbor republics (1 Chronicles 4:41-43).[34]

Wines' argument shows us the right of a *county* to defend its boundaries. It also shows that several such counties can band together to fight an aggressor. A nation may do so as well. Is there anything wrong, then, with a group of nations banding together to fight an aggressor? Clearly not. The Christian nations of Europe were forced repeatedly to ally together to fight the Turk. Such alliances were temporary, but it was recognized that the Turk threatened Christendom in her entirety and that everyone's welfare was at stake.

Similarly, throughout most of the 20th century, the Soviet Union was openly declaring its intention to subvert and conquer all the Christian nations of the world. While hostilities only occasionally broke out, this Cold War continued for well over fifty years. It is entirely appropriate

---

34 E. C. Wines, *Commentaries on the Laws of the Ancient Hebrews* (Philadelphia, Pa.: Presbyterian Board of Publication, 1853; reprinted: Powder Springs, Ga.: American Vision, 2009), 505f.

for Christian nations to band together to fight such a menace to Christendom. Today, resurgent Islam poses a threat of similar if not greater proportions.

This discussion expands our notion of boundaries. There are county boundaries that can be defended by war. There are larger, national boundaries that must also be defended. There are also *international boundaries* that must be defended. Isolationist sentiment, reacting against modern secular "one-world" views of alliances, sometimes fails to take this into account.

MATURATION AND COMPLEXITY

As a person grows and matures, he becomes more complex. His relationships with people and with the world become richer and more diversified. The problems he faces become more subtle. Once he heard the rule: "Don't set foot in the street, son." Now, as an adult, he faces tougher, more complicated problems.

The same thing is true of the human race. God has designed the world to grow in diversity and complexity, in richness and splendor. The New Testament tells us that people in the ancient world, including Israel, were like children. God kept them from having to face complicated, mature situations. He kept it relatively simple for them. Paul writes:

> Now I say, as long as the heir is a child, he does not differ at all from a slave, although he is owner of everything, but he is under guardians and managers until the date set by the father. So we too, when we were children, were held in bondage under the elementary principles of the world. (Gal. 4:1-3, NASB)

Paul is not saying that "man has come of age" in the sense that certain modernist theologians have used this phrase. He is not saying we can ignore the Old Testament or put aside God's law in favor of "situation ethics." He is simply saying that there is a maturing process at work in humanity just as there is in individuals.

This point is important for us as we consider warfare. In the ancient world, prior to the rise of the great empires, war was pretty simple. One day an army of soldiers and chariots invades your land. You defend on the battlefield. You may have to hole up in a city behind walls. After a few battles, one side or the other is massacred, and the war is over. Their nation is pretty small, and so is yours.

Modern war is not like that. There is no place to hide from modern weapons, nor is there any limit to their range. Moreover, the enemy of God, Satanic humanism, has become more subtle. We don't face sweeping hordes of Amalekites. The enemy has more effective tools at his disposal.

In the ancient world there was no printing press, no radio, no television. This means there was really no such thing as propaganda and brainwashing. Now there is. It is a harder weapon to deal with, in terms of "cold war."

In the ancient world, travel was long and arduous. Nations far away were no threat. You only had to worry about the people next door. That is no longer the case. It is easy to think about dealing with a neighboring aggressor nation, but what do you do with a nation halfway around the globe that is using all kinds of subtle tricks to defeat you? What if that nation halfway around the globe is filling the nation right next to you with hate-propaganda? Do you counter it with your own? Do you sit silently and ignore it? Do you create "Radio Christian Europe" and beam into the Islamic world lots of counter-propaganda? And who is "you"? The national government? A body of churches?

In the ancient world, people did not know one another well. Modern techniques for learning other languages and cultures did not exist. As a result, there was little spying. Now there is much. Trained spies and traitors are part and parcel of modern war.

One way to handle this matter is to take enemy statements seriously. When Nikita Khrushchëv said, "We will bury you," perhaps the United States should simply have declared war and destroyed the U.S.S.R. right then and there. Khrushchëv had certainly announced once again the Soviet intention to conquer the West. If that is not a declaration of war, what is?

So, why not just go to war? Well, because of nuclear weapons. We really don't want to run the risk of destroying our whole nation and perhaps our entire world civilization. We'd rather fight in subtler ways and avoid a nuclear holocaust. So then, we are back to the complexity of the modern world.

In George Washington's day it was much easier to "ignore Europe" than it is today. Our modern "global situation" forces the United States to be more cognizant of international affairs than our forefathers needed to be. It is still true that each nation should mind its own business, but its "business" has increased.

Christians sometimes think that they can sit in armchairs and criticize all the day-to-day decisions made by their governments. Actually, most of us, myself included, are not privy to enough information about what is really going on in the world to do more than speak in general terms about principles—which is all I am doing in these essays. What we can do, however, is ask God to give us sane, wise, Christian leaders who will operate in terms of biblical principles as they lead our nation through the treacherous waters of "cold warfare."

CONCLUSION

We have seen that the principle of boundary means that each cultural nation as well as each civil state should mind its own business. It means additionally that each human society, whether the home, a locale, or a larger governmental unit, has a right of self-defense against aggression. Finally, we discussed the fact that boundaries exist at several levels, including an "international boundary" between groups of friendly Christian powers and hostile pagan ones.

International Alliances

"You shall make no covenant with them or with their gods."
— Exod. 23:32 (New American Standard Version)

"Woe to the rebellious children," declares the Lord, "who execute a plan, but not Mine, and make an alliance, but not of My Spirit, in order to add sin to sin."
— Isa. 30:1 (New American Standard Version)

The three Persons of God are allied together. Theologians sometimes speak of this relationship as a "covenant." In addition to being One in "essence," the three Persons of God are covenanted or bonded together. They thus represent the ultimate "Holy Alliance."

Men are either allied with God in covenant or they are set against Him as enemies. There is no neutral ground. Moreover, all those allied with God are allied with each other in the unity of the Church. Finally, it is obvious that no alliance can be made between Christian and pagan, between God's people and His enemies.

The Bible teaches the same thing regarding the nations. There is a proper place for alliances and treaties between Christian nations, but there is no place for alliances between Christians and pagans. It is our purpose in this essay to explore this dimension of international relations.

FORBIDDEN ALLIANCES

When Israel came out of Egypt, God strictly forbade them to enter into any kinds of treaties or alliances with the people of Canaan: "You shall make no covenant with them or with their gods" (Exod. 23:32; compare Exod. 34:12; Deut. 7:2).

It is sometimes assumed that these laws teach that God does not want nations to ally together for any purposes, that no nation has any concerns outside its own borders. Some say the Bible forbids any and all "entangling alliances."

This is not a correct interpretation, however. What these passages clearly forbid is any alliance with idolatry, with any pagan nation. They do not prohibit alliances with other faithful nations. Some kind of alliance came into being between Moses' Israel and Jethro's Midian (Exodus 18).

All the same, the Bible has much to say against alliances with pagan nations. Christians are not to be unequally yoked with unbelievers in marriage or religious activities (2 Cor. 6:14), and this same principle applies to nations. Israel was obviously not to make any alliances with the Canaanites, since she was to destroy them utterly. By implication, no alliances were to be made with any pagan nations.

Concerning the kings of Israel, the law of God commanded, "And he shall not acquire many wives for himself, so that his heart does not turn away; nor shall he greatly increase silver and gold for himself." (Deut. 17:17, NASB). Since polygamy was already strictly forbidden in the law (Lev. 18:18), we need to ask why God would bother to give this rule specifically for kings.[35] The answer is that such royal marriages were alliances.

The premier example of this sin of marital alliances is Solomon. The climax of the good side of the story of Solomon is the visit of Queen Sheba (1 Kings 10:1-13). This story shows the conversion of a Gentile nation and an exchange of gifts between the leaders of two Godly peoples. Immediately after this story, we are shown Solomon breaking the Three Laws of Kingship, found in Deut.17:16-17.

First, Solomon aggrandized the state by multiplying gold to himself: "Now the weight of gold that came to Solomon in one year was 666 talents of gold" (1 Kings 10:14, NASB). Does the number 666 remind you of anything? One table of moneys, weights, and measures says that a talent of gold would be equivalent to $5,760,000.00 in 1985 American

---

35 Lev. 18:18 says, "And you shall not marry a woman in addition to her sister as a second wife while she is alive, to uncover her nakedness." (NASB). This law prohibits all polygamy. In the ancient world, if a man was of a mind to take a second wife, he might think first of his wife's sister. Remember what happened to Jacob. By prohibiting a man from marrying two sisters, the law forbids all polygamy. Moreover, the Bible frequently speaks of all believers as brothers and sisters, and this law really means "any other woman," not just a blood-sister. Finally, the reason given for not taking a second wife is so that the "nakedness" of the first is not uncovered.

This means, so that the first wife is not put to shame (naked = ashamed; Gen. 2:25; 3:7). As mentioned before, to take a second wife is like announcing to the world that the first is inadequate.

Additionally, Gen.2:24 says that a man shall "cleave" ("cling or stick to") to his wife. If he cleaves to her, he will not be able to cleave to another, which by implication rules out polygamy and adultery.

There is confusion on this point because so many important people in the Bible sinned by taking more than one wife. If you did take a second wife, you were not allowed to give her away. You had to keep her. That is, once you get into a polygamous relationship, there is no way back out. You just have to suffer the consequences, and every polygamist in the Bible is shown to suffer quite dramatically.

dollars.³⁶ This comes to $3,836,160,000.00 per 1985 year for Solomon, or $8,684,945,023.00 per 2017 year, almost nine billion dollars. Assuming for the sake of argument that these figures are correct, that's a pretty hefty budget for an empire in the ancient world.

Second, Solomon built up a large aggressive war machine by importing horses from Egypt (1 Kings 10:28-29).

Third, Solomon formed alliances by marrying foreign women: "seven hundred wives, who were princesses, and three hundred concubines; and his wives turned his heart away" (1 Kings 11:3, NASB).³⁷ He allowed the gods of the nations each to have a sanctuary within Israel (1 Kings 11:7-8).

Solomon had sought to increase strength and security by making false alliances with pagan nations. God made the punishment fit the crime: Solomon's very actions would cause his empire to collapse and his nation to divide in two. God would put into effect the principle of the Tower of Babel.

God said, "You want to maintain a big, aggressive war machine? I'll give you war!" So, "Yahweh raised up an adversary against Solomon, Hadad the Edomite" (1 Kings 11:14, NASB). Then, "God also raised up another adversary against him, Rezon the son of Eliada" (1 Kings 11:23,

---

36 *The King James Open Bible: Expanded Edition* (Nashville, Tenn.: Thomas Nelson Publishers, 1985).

37 James B. Jordan, *The Law of the Covenant: An Exposition of Exodus 21-23* (Tyler, Tex.: Institute for Christian Economics, 1984), 84ff., 146ff. A concubine was not a mistress or a kept woman. Rather, a concubine was a true wife, entitled to all the privileges of marriage (Exod. 22:7-11). The difference between a concubine and a first-class wife was that the first-class wife came to the marriage with a "dowry" that gave her independent wealth and power, while the concubine was totally dependent on the husband and thus in a reduced status. My book is out of print but may be found online.

NASB). Alliances with pagans make God angry. Alliances with pagans do not ensure peace; they ensure that God will bring war.

God said, "You want unity through taxation? I'll show you how much unity taxation brings!" So, the Lord raised up Jeroboam to bring civil war to Israel and eventually to lead a secession (1 Kings 11:26-40).

Massive centralized government makes God angry. Massive centralized government does not bring unity; it ensures that God will act to cause division. Remember the Tower of Babel.

We might think Israel would learn from Solomon, but they did not. In 2 Chronicles 16, we find the story of King Asa. Asa was king of Judah, or Southern Israel. He started out very well, reforming the nation and leading the people back to the Lord. In his old age, however, he forgot the truth. "In the thirty-sixth year of Asa's reign, Baasha king of Israel came up against Judah and fortified Ramah in order to prevent anyone from going out or coming in to Asa king of Judah" (2 Chron. 16:1, NASB). At this point, Asa should have trusted God, organized his army, and dealt with Baasha. Instead, however, Asa made a deal with pagans:

> Then Asa brought out silver and gold from the treasuries of the house of the Lord and the king's house, and sent it to Ben-hadad king of Aram, who lived in Damascus, saying, "A treaty must be made between you and me, as there was between my father and your father. Behold, I have sent you silver and gold; go, break your treaty with Baasha king of Israel so that he will withdraw from me." (2 Chron. 16:2-3, NASB)

Now, except for taking gold from God's temple, this certainly looks like a reasonable ploy. It is the kind of thing the U.S. State Department and CIA do every day. And it worked, as the following verses show: Ben-Hadad turned against Northern Israel and Baasha left Asa and Judah alone. But God cursed Asa for it:

> At that time Hanani the seer came to Asa king of Judah and said to him, "Because you have relied on the king of Aram and have not relied on the Lord your God, for that reason the army of the king of Aram has escaped from your hand. Were not the Ethiopians and the Lubim an immense army with very many chariots and horsemen? Yet because you relied on the Lord, He handed them over to you. For the eyes of the Lord roam throughout the earth, so that He may strongly support those whose heart is completely His. You have acted foolishly in this. Indeed, from now on you will have wars" (2 Chron. 16:7-9, NASB)

Does God really exist? Is He the living God of the Bible who is involved in the affairs of nations? Or is He some Great Being of the philosophers, just the Big Idea? If God really *lives*, then we need to take Him into account in our foreign policy.

Jehoshaphat was the Godly son of Asa, but he did not learn the lesson. He formed an alliance with ungodly Ahab by marrying Ahab's daughter (2 Chron. 18:1). After a disastrous war that Ahab got him into, described in 2 Chronicles 18, Jehoshaphat was warned by Hanani: "Should you help the wicked and love those who hate Yahweh?" (2 Chron. 19:2, NASB).

Jehoshaphat listened to the prophet, and when Moab and Ammon made war against him, he formed no alliances with anyone else. Instead he prayed to God, gathered his army, and God gave him the victory (2 Chron. 20:1-30). The result: "And the dread of God was on all the kingdoms of the lands when they heard that Yahweh had fought against the enemies of Israel." (2 Chron. 20:29, NASB).

Then Jehoshaphat forgot.

> After this Jehoshaphat king of Judah allied himself with Ahaziah king of Israel. He acted wickedly [a]in so doing. So he allied himself with him to make ships to go to Tarshish, and they made the ships in Ezion-geber. Then Eliezer the son of Dodavahu of Mareshah prophesied against Jehoshaphat, saying, "Because you have allied yourself with Ahaziah, the Lord has destroyed your works." So the ships were wrecked and could not go to Tarshish. (2 Chron. 20:35-37, NASB)

Is it ever appropriate to enter into a treaty with a pagan nation? Yes, *if such a treaty is to guarantee or establish a boundary.* Such treaties are precisely for the purpose of *separation*, not union. An example is found in Gen. 31:43-55. Jacob formed a treaty with Laban, and these were the terms: "This heap is a witness, and the memorial stone is a witness, that I will not pass by this heap to you for harm, and you will not pass by this heap and this memorial stone to me, for harm" (Gen. 31:52, NASB). We see from this that such boundary agreements are entirely proper. This has relevance to such modern problems as freedom of the seas, as we see in Chapter 12.

In summary, God does not permit alliances between Christian and pagan nations either for the purpose of defense or for common works projects. Only boundary agreements are permitted.

THE ISRAELITE ALLIANCE

Before looking at the question of international alliances, we need to consider the situation in Israel itself. While from one point of view Israel was one nation, from another point of view Israel was a permanent alliance or confederacy of separate states. We have seen in the preceding chapter that each Israelite tribe or county could make war on its own. E. C. Wines summarizes the broader picture when he writes:

> It is agreed on all hands by those who have written on the Hebrew institutes, that each tribe formed a separate state. Each composed an entire political community, in some respects independent of the others. Each was under its own proper government, administered its own affairs by its own representative assemblies and magistrates, and claimed and exercised many of the rights of sovereignty. Its local legislation and municipal arrangements were in its own hands.... It is evident that every tribe had its own prince and judge, and that every prince or head of a tribe judged his own people; consequently every tribe had a sceptre and lawgiver, as well as the tribe of Judah.[38]

There was, of course, a true national union in Israel as well, but it was a union built upon confederation. Wines states that "there were four departments of the Hebrew government: viz, the chief magistrate, whether judge, high priest, or king; the senate of princes; the congregation or Israel, the popular branch of the government; and the oracle of Jehovah [that is, the Church—J.B.J.]...."[39] In his valuable study, Wines devotes a chapter to each of these departments.

This national union was, however, fundamentally religious. It was entirely possible for tribes to secede from the political union without breaking the religious union. The tribes had in common one set of moral and civil principles (the revealed Law of God), and they were involved in one Church (particularly in the three annual festivals). Engagement in *political* union was entirely *voluntary*. Certain key events in the history of Israel make this point clear.

Let us look first of all at Joshua 22. Here we find that when the land of Canaan was settled, the tribes of Reuben, Gad, and half of Manasseh settled on the eastern side of the

---

38 Wines, *Commentaries*, 504

39 Ibid., 490.

Jordan river. After the land was pacified, these three tribes built an altar by the Jordan, "a large altar in appearance" (Joshua 22:10). The ten tribes on the west side of the Jordan interpreted this action to mean that the eastern tribes were setting up a new religion in competition with the Tabernacle. They gathered themselves for war and confronted Reuben, Gad, and Manasseh.

The three trans-Jordanian tribes replied that they had built this altar not for any purpose of worship, but as a symbol of religious and national unity. They said they had built it out of fear:

> "...but truly we have done this out of concern, for a reason, saying, 'In time to come your sons may say to our sons, "What have you to do with Yahweh, the God of Israel? For Yahweh has made the Jordan a border between us and you, you sons of Reuben and sons of Gad; you have no portion in Yahweh" So your sons may make our sons stop fearing Yahweh. Therefore we said, 'Let's build an altar, not for burnt offering or for sacrifice; rather, it shall be a witness between us and you and between our generations after us.'" (Josh. 22:24-27, NASB)

We see from this incident that the union of the tribes was grounded in religion, not in a political order. Politically speaking, Israel was a confederacy.

The second story that shows the nature of Israel's political union is found in 2 Samuel 2. We read that after the death of King Saul, "Then the men of Judah came, and there they anointed David king over the house of Judah" (2 Sam. 2:4, NASB). Two very important facts emerge from this verse.

First, it is clear that the king in Israel was an elective office. It is true that God later established the house of David as a dynasty, but that was a special act of God. The normal procedure was election. Moreover, David had already been set aside by God as Israel's future king (1 Sam. 16:1-13), yet even so, it was still necessary for the people to establish him in office by election.

Second, it is clear that David was not simply a tribal prince but a true king, though reigning only over one tribe at this point. The rest of Israel was ruled by Saul's son:

> But Abner the son of Ner, commander of Saul's army, had taken Ish-bosheth the son of Saul and brought him over to Mahanaim. And he made him king over Gilead, over the Ashurites, over Jezreel, over Ephraim, and over Benjamin, even over all Israel. Ish-bosheth, Saul's son, was forty years old when he became king over Israel, and he was king for two years. The house of Judah, however, followed David. (2 Sam. 2:8-10, NASB)

At this point there were two kings and two political confederations within the one Israelite nation. If there had been one political confederation with one king, then Judah would have been part of the confederation, and David would simply have been the prince of Judah. David would have been under Ishbosheth as king over all Israel. This was not the case. Judah was separate and independent from the rest of the nation. Judah had its own king, and the rest of Israel had another king. Each king was thoroughly legitimate and constitutional.

David made no move to conquer the rest of Israel. He simply waited until the remaining tribes were ready to join with Judah in a new confederation. War did break out, of course, but it was not because of David's doing. The actual aggression came from Abner, commander of Ishbosheth's army: "Now Abner the son of Ner, went from Mahanaim to Gibeon with the servants of Ish-bosheth the son of Saul" (2 Sam. 2:12, NASB). Gibeon was a city in Benjamin near the border of Judah. Abner brought an army there, and this was a direct challenge to the sovereign state of Judah.

Unfortunately, David was saddled to a violent and bloodthirsty commander of his own, Joab, who lacked the wisdom to avoid this confrontation. (On Joab, see 2 Sam. 3:22-39; 1 Kings 2:5-6.) Joab crossed the border and went to meet Abner. Each side chose champions to fight in a contest to see whose army was stronger. The Lord brought it to pass that "each one of them seized his opponent by the head and thrust his sword in his opponent's side; so they fell down together" (2 Sam. 2:16, NASB). Thus, the Lord showed them that both sides were equal in His eyes and neither should try to conquer the other. A battle broke out, however, and war ensued—a war that David regretted to his dying days (1 Kings 2:5-6).

Once it became apparent that David's side was going to win the war, two of Ishbosheth's military captains murdered their king in his bed and brought his head to David (2 Sam. 4:1-8). David's response to this murder was to have the two men hanged and to give Ishbosheth proper burial as an honored king (2 Sam. 4:9-12). The point we draw from this, once again, is that it was entirely proper and constitutional for there to be two separate kingdoms in the one nation of Israel. David honored this principle, even though Joab did not.

After this, all the other tribes came to David and made him their king (2 Sam. 5:3). Here again we see that the political union in the nation was confederate in nature, a political alliance.

A final story that brings out this principle of alliance and confederation is found in 1 Kings 12. After Solomon's death, his son Rehoboam came to the throne of all Israel. The nation assembled to ask Rehoboam to lighten his taxes. Rehoboam refused to do so, and the ten northern tribes seceded under Jeroboam. God Himself had authorized Jeroboam to lead this secession if necessary (1 Kings 11:26-39). The northern tribes established Jeroboam as king.

When Rehoboam gathered his army to try to force the northern tribes back into the Davidic confederacy, God forbade him from doing so (1 Kings 12:21-24).

This political secession was completely legitimate and non-revolutionary. Of course, Jeroboam was not content with political secession. He established a new religion with new festivals in order to try and shatter the *religious* union of the people, and for this God cursed him (1 Kings 12:25 - 14:20).

What emerges from this is that there is nothing wrong with Christian states forming a confederacy with an overarching political government. On the other hand, there is nothing wrong with Christian states seceding from such a confederation whenever they wish.

ALLIANCES WITH OTHER NATIONS

Of course, it is true that the temporary political union of the Israelite counties under David and Solomon was the union of one nation of people. It was not a political union among several nations or peoples. At the same time, there is no reason under the New Covenant not to extend the principles of the Hebrew confederacy to all Christian nations. If the Christian nations of Europe once wished to join in recognizing one "Holy Roman Emperor" for certain limited purposes (defense against the Turks, for instance), there is nothing wrong with this, in principle.

Such alliances among nations are usually temporary and for certain specific purposes. Do we see examples of this in the Bible? Certainly. Before we summarize these, however, we need to clear up a common misconception about the Old Testament. Many people think that God did not save anyone except Israelites after the call of Abraham. If you wanted to be saved, you had to become a Jew.

Actually, this was what the Pharisees believed. We see examples of Gentile believers in the New Testament (Acts 10), and we also see them in the Old Testament as well. Israel was called to act as *priests* to the nations, but this peculiar calling did not mean only Israel was saved. Actually, when Israel did her job salvation was extended to many nations. Remember the Queen of Sheba. The fundamental principle set out in the Abrahamic Covenant in this regard was this: "And I will bless those who bless you, and the one who curses you I will curse. And in you all the families of the earth will be blessed" (Gen. 12:3, NASB).

The Book of Genesis shows this principle played out repeatedly. When Pharaoh of Egypt attacked Sarah, God cursed him (Gen. 12:10-20). Later, God cursed Abimelech of Philistia for the same sin (Genesis 20). On the other hand, once Abimelech came to his senses and converted (Gen. 20:3ff.), Abraham was willing to enter into a limited covenant—alliance—with him (Gen. 21:22-34). This same story played out again with a new Abimelech and Isaac (Genesis 26).

The most dramatic fulfillment of the Abrahamic Covenant in Genesis happens at the end, however, with the conversion of Pharaoh and Egypt. This conversion is recorded in Genesis 41, where Pharaoh submits himself to the Word of God and blesses Joseph by setting him over Egypt. After this, we see Pharaoh and his servants always rejoicing at the good things that happen to Joseph and his family (Gen. 45:16ff.; 47:5ff.). Indeed, in explicit fulfillment of the Abrahamic promise, we find that when Jacob was presented before Pharaoh, Pharaoh knelt to receive Jacob's blessing (Gen. 47:7, 10).

Joseph married the daughter of the chief priest of Heliopolis, thus entering into an alliance with the converted Egyptians (Gen. 41:45). And of course, a very close political alliance is implied by the fact that Egypt gave Israel the land of Goshen in which to live. (Later on, as we know, Egypt apostatized from the Lord and began to persecute Israel.)

The Bible does not tell us a great deal about the conversion of Gentile nations, but the book of Jonah stands as the enduring proof that such conversions did happen. Moreover, a reading of the history of David shows men of many nations joining themselves to David's household, the most famous being Uriah the *Hittite*.

One final passage can be noted along these lines. After Lot was captured by Chedorlaomer, we read: "Then a survivor came and told Abram the Hebrew. Now he was residing by the oaks of Mamre the Amorite, brother of Eshcol and brother of Aner, and *they were allies with Abram*" (Gen. 14:13, NASB; italics mine). The language here clearly implies some form of alliance with these other Godly sheikhs. (Scholars have estimated that Sheikh Abraham probably had about 3000 persons in his household, based on the fact that he had 318 warriors in his retinue [Gen. 14:14]. Thus, such an alliance was no small matter.)[40]

PROPER AND IMPROPER ALLIANCES

In this section we want to take up the question of alliances and entanglements between Christian and non-Christian nations. We shall discuss two principles. The first is that Christian nations are never to *initiate* alliances with non-Christian nations. The second is that Christians are not to give aid and assistance to those who hate the Lord.

As we have seen, God forbids Christian nations to trust in alliances with pagans. In times of distress we are to place our trust in Him, not in detente with false gods. We looked

---

40 James B. Jordan, *The Sociology of the Church: Essays in Reconstruction* (Tyler, Texas: Geneva Ministries, 1986; reprint Eugene: Wipf and Stock, 1999). See Chapter 3 for a fuller discussion of the salvation of the Gentiles in the Old Covenant.

at the stories of Kings Asa and Jehoshaphat (2 Chronicles 16 and 20) and found that God brought judgment against these leaders when they initiated alliances with the ungodly.

Does this mean that Christian nations can have absolutely nothing to do with helping non-Christian nations against a common enemy? Not at all. It is a matter of who initiates the deal and what the terms of the deal include.

A key passage is in Genesis 26: "Then Abimelech came to him from Gerar with his adviser Ahuzzath, and Phicol the commander of his army...they said, 'We have seen plainly that the Lord has been with you; so we said, "An oath must now be taken by us," that is, by you and us. So let us make a covenant with you'" (Gen. 26:26, 28, NASB). Notice that it was the Gentiles who asked Isaac for an alliance, not the other way around. Similarly, in Gen. 21:22-34, we find that the Philistines had earlier initiated a covenant with Abraham. *They* asked for the covenant or alliance. *They* sued for terms. *They* accepted the conditions set forth by Abraham and Isaac.

A later illustration of this principle is found in Joshua 9. During the conquest of Canaan, one of the Canaanite tribes, the Gibeonites, decided that slavery was preferable to liquidation. They disguised themselves and met with Joshua and his men. They pretended to be travelers from a far country and sued for an alliance.

After making a covenant of peace with them, the Israelites learned that the Gibeonites were in fact Canaanites, whom they were supposed to destroy. Having sworn before the Lord, however, the Israelites could not break their oath. They did not destroy the Gibeonites, but did place them in a subordinate status as "woodcutters and water carriers."

Now let's make an application to the modern world. Let's assume that the Netherlands undergoes a revival and once again becomes a Christian nation. Let's assume that Algeria becomes a major threat to Europe. Would it be right for the Netherlands to try to form an alliance with the secular humanist states of Europe in order to resist militant Islam? No. We are commanded to trust in the Lord and not to seek help from the heathen.

Suppose the European states seek help from the Netherlands? Is Holland allowed to help them? Yes, because they have come to the believing nation, instead of the believers coming to them. The believers can even create a treaty or alliance with them, on proper terms. In this way, we Christians do not become involved in "entangling" alliances because we remain in control.

What kinds of terms must we require? The rule here is what the prophet Hanani said to King Jehoshaphat: "Should you help the wicked and love those who hate Yahweh?" (2 Chron. 19:2, NASB). Not only must we avoid becoming entangled with pagan nations, we must also avoid becoming entangled in a fight with the Lord. Our actions as a nation must be pleasing to Him.

Now, since the pagan nation is coming to us for help, we can set the terms. For instance, we can require that Christian missionaries be free and unhindered; otherwise, no deal. For years and years, evangelical Christians knew that the most closed nation on earth, as far as the gospel is concerned, was Afghanistan. Missionaries were not permitted into Afghanistan at all. Then the Lord gave the Western nations a golden opportunity. "You want our help against the Soviets? All right, but you have to let in the missionaries."

This principle applies, obviously, not only to more formal alliances, but also to any kind of foreign aid. Foreign aid must never go to help the enemies of the Lord. It must always have strings attached. Otherwise it is simply subsidizing evil.

As we shall see in Chapter 12, the two best ways of accomplishing foreign aid, such as relief to the starving, are through the Church and through free trade. Caring for the needy is primarily the Church's job, and a policy of free trade means that money will flow from "have" nations to "have not" nations, provided the "have not" nations work hard and earn it. Everyone benefits from such a policy, and the civil government can remain out of the arrangement entirely.

Suppose a foreign nation approaches our Christian government and wants some kind of help? The question we would have to ask is, "What are you willing to give in exchange?" If they want us to provide them with weapons or spare parts, perhaps we will want them to provide us with access to their intelligence reports. The military can negotiate these arrangements to the satisfaction of both parties.

The Bible tells us that the primary duty of the civil government is the maintenance of order by the use of the sword (Romans 13). Charity and relief are not the normal business of the state. Practically, this means that if a foreign nation wants to negotiate some kind of benefit from us, the military branch of our government should be consulted. If our military can see some benefit or can formulate some reasonable deal, then such an arrangement would be a proper function of the state. In other words, any foreign aid flowing from the coffers of the civil magistracy should be related to defense. Otherwise, foreign aid should be the business of the Church and private associations.

CONCLUSION

International relations are multifaceted and often complex, but for the Christian two principles stand out. The first is that the Christian nation must always deal from strength.

In times of trouble we must seek an alliance with the Lord, not with the heathen nations around us. If they want to ally with us, then we must set the terms. We must never seek to ally with them.

The second principle is that we must never assist or finance those who openly oppose the Lord and His purposes on the earth. If they want our help, then we can give it, but only if they permit the gospel to go forth unhindered in their land.

It is proper for Christian nations to form mutual defense pacts to defend the common borders of Christendom against anti-Christian aggressors. In *principle*, there is nothing wrong and everything right with alliances designed to protect Christian nations from the modern Turk of resurgent Islam.

In fact, however, such alliances as NATO are secular humanist alliances, not Christian ones. The United States of America and the other previously Christian nations are governed today not by Christian principles but by pagan ones. Until our nations are restored to biblical principles of government, such alliances will not be blessed by God and will prove ineffective. We return to this problem in Chapter 9.

United States Foreign Policy: Some Observations

In this essay we discuss some aspects of American foreign policy in the light of the principles we have set out in the preceding chapters. We are covering four general areas: first, a discussion of the purpose of foreign policy; second, a brief history of American international involvements; third, how we should deal with international communism and the cold war; and fourth, the question of foreign aid.

Though this essay is being published for a universal Christian audience, I shall use the United States as an example for inspection because I am most familiar with it.

THE PURPOSE OF FOREIGN POLICY

Conservatives and conservative Christians sometimes assume that the goal of foreign policy is national survival. This can be right or wrong, depending on what is meant by *survival*.

As we have seen, God clearly desires for there to be many nations on the earth, each glorifying Him in its own unique ways. On the other hand, there are times when a given nation becomes so corrupt that God eliminates it totally, as with the world before the Flood and the Canaanites. These two historical incidents are continual reminders to Christians that not every nation deserves to survive, and not every nation has been able to.

The prophet Jeremiah was given a message that was very unpopular with the conservatives of his day:

> In the beginning of the reign of Zedekiah the son of Josiah, king of Judah, this word came to Jeremiah from the Lord, saying— this is what the Lord has said to me: "Make for yourself restraints and yokes and put them on your neck, and send word to the king of Edom, the king of Moab, the king of the sons of Ammon, the king of Tyre, and to the king of Sidon by the messengers who come to Jerusalem to Zedekiah king of Judah. Order them to go to their masters, saying, 'This is what the Lord of armies, the God of Israel says: "This is what you shall say to your masters: 'I have made the earth, mankind, and the animals which are on the face of the earth by My great power and by My outstretched arm, and I will give it to the one who is pleasing in My sight. And now I have handed all these lands over to Nebuchadnezzar king of Babylon, My servant, and I have also given him the animals of the field to serve him. All the nations shall serve him and his son and his grandson until the time of his own land comes; then many nations and great kings will make him their servant. 'And it will be that the nation or the kingdom which will not serve him, Nebuchadnezzar king of Babylon, and will not put its neck under the yoke of the king of Babylon, I will punish that nation with the sword, with famine, and with plague,' declares the Lord, 'until I have eliminated it by his hand. And as for you, do not listen to your prophets, your diviners, your dreamers, your soothsayers, or your sorcerers who talk to you, saying, "You will not serve the king of Babylon." For they are prophesying a lie to you in order to remove you far from your land; and I will drive

> you away and you will perish. But the nation that will bring its neck under the yoke of the king of Babylon and serve him, I will let remain on its land,' declares the Lord, 'and they will cultivate it and live in it.'"'" I spoke words like all these to Zedekiah king of Judah, saying, "Bring your necks under the yoke of the king of Babylon and serve him and his people, and live! (Jer. 27:1-12, NASB)

This was not a very popular message. Suppose Russia attacked the United States and defeated it in several battles. Then the leading clergy in the United States united to counsel surrender because God was punishing the USA for its sins. How popular would that be with the American people?

The interesting thing to notice is that Jeremiah's counsel was designed precisely for national survival. If they continued to fight Nebuchadnezzar, he said, then that king would deport them and spread them all over the world. If they surrendered, however, then while the Israelite *government* would die, the Israelite *nation and people* would remain intact and would eventually be restored.

In other words, Jeremiah counseled a judicial surrender as a strategy for national survival. He was able to give this counsel because what mattered to him was not the state (the ruler), but the nation.

In discussing the purpose of foreign policy, then, we have to insist that the purpose of every specific nation is the glory of God. As we have seen, each nation is to glorify God in its own way, and that means national survival, the protection of boundaries, and so forth. Additionally, the glory of God may mean that nations must band together to resist common anti-Christian enemies. And, finally, the Christian statesman may find himself, like Jeremiah, forced to agree with the judgment of God against his own nation.

A nation may have to suffer a temporary eclipse of prestige and independence in order to ensure its long-term survival as a Godly society.

UNITED STATES INTERNATIONAL INVOLVEMENT

For the first century after the War of Independence, the United States essentially ignored international affairs. It was busy with internal disputes and "taming" (conquering) the West. Around the 1890s, however, the United States government began to become more and more involved overseas. Initially, Americans were not very interested in Europe, however, for several reasons. It was widely believed that America was a new, progressive order in the world, while Europe was regarded as old and decadent. Moreover, European powers, especially England, had sided against the United States during the War of Independence and the Napoleonic Wars (the American "War of 1812") and had tended to support the Confederacy in the American Civil War, or the War Between the States.

Finally, at this time the United States was simply invulnerable from European attack and thus could easily ignore Europe.

Regarding Latin America and the Far East the situation was different. Four large factors moved the United States into an imperialistic posture toward the end of the 1800s. First:

> "...the shifting intellectual currents of the times altered the attitudes of Americans toward foreign affairs. Darwin's theories, applicable by analogy to international relations, gave the concept of manifest destiny a new plausibility.

> Darwinists like the historian John Fiske argued that the American democratic system of government was clearly the world's 'fittest' and must spread inevitably over 'every land on the earth's surface.'"[41]

Other Darwinists argued that the Anglo-Saxon race was the fittest, and that American Anglo-Saxons were thus destined to rule the world.[42]

Second, European countries had already gobbled up and divided Africa and were doing the same in the Far East. Some Americans wanted to join the feast before all the choicest lands had been devoured.

Third, after the Civil War, the U.S. Navy had been virtually disbanded and her ships were rusting away. The Navy wanted a reason to keep itself going. Accordingly, Commodore Stephen B. Luce began to promote the ideas of Captain Alfred Thayer Mahan, who developed:

> "...a startling theory about the importance of sea power, which he explained to the public in two important books, *The Influence of Sea Power upon History* (1980) and *The Influence of Sea Power upon the French Revolution and Empire* (1892). History proved, according to Mahan, that a nation with a powerful navy and the overseas bases necessary to maintain it would be both invulnerable in war and prosperous in time of peace. Applied to the current American situation, Mahan explained in a series of magazine articles, this meant that in addition to building a modern fleet, the United States should obtain a string of coaling stations and bases in the Caribbean, annex the Hawaiian Islands, and cut a canal across Central America. Eventually a more extensive colonial empire might follow. . . ."[43]

---

41 John A. Garraty, *The American Nation: A History of the United States* (New York, N.Y.: Harper & Row, 1966), 623.

42 Ibid., 623f.

43 Ibid., 624.

Fourth, wealthy monied interests, operating as they usually do behind the scenes, were interested in the profits to be made via imperialistic exploitation. The full story on such "conspiracies" can probably never be fully known, but no one disputes the contention that wealthy financial interests in England and Europe had their counterparts in the United States, and all saw opportunities to expand their wealth through the development of colonial empires.[44]

During the 1890s, because of pressures from the imperialists in the United States, the American government entered an immoral war with Spain and acquired the Philippines, greatly expanded its presence in the Caribbean, and began to meddle more and more in affairs in China and the rest of the Far East. Anti-imperialist conservatives opposed all this, but were unable to stop it. This was the first big change in American foreign policy: imperialistic expansion into the Far East and Latin America. The second came with World War I.

The attitude of Americans toward Germany and England has always been ambivalent. On the one hand, anti-English feeling was always present because of the War of Independence, the War of 1812, and English neutrality regarding the Confederacy during the American Civil War. On the other hand, Americans saw themselves as Anglo-Saxons, and thus culturally linked with England. To this day, the American popular press follows the shenanigans of the English royal house, paying scant attention to that of the Netherlands by comparison.

At the same time, Americans have traditionally been somewhat in awe of the German intellectual life. Americans erroneously think that German is *the* language of scholarship. They think of the history of music, for example,

---

[44] Carroll Quigley, *Tragedy and Hope: A History of the World in Our Time* (New York, N.Y.: Macmillan, 1966).

as the history of German/Austrian music. Most Americans would enjoy the nine symphonies of Antonin Dvorak more than the Beethoven nine, but few ever think of it.

Whether it is theology, the arts, or the sciences, Americans think the Germans know the most. Why side with England against Germany in World War I then? A good question, the answer to which has to do with the effectiveness of English propaganda during the early years of the war. Conservative and Christian historians have condemned England for helping provoke World War I because of England's basic foreign policy: the maintenance of a balance of power. The basic purpose of British diplomacy was this maintenance of the "balance of power," which meant in practice that Britain would act to keep everyone at each other's throats so that Britain could come out ahead. Britain would side with the weaker party to help tear down anyone who was getting too strong. At any rate, while there was plenty of fault on all sides in World War I, the hostilities in Europe had nothing to do with the United States. Nevertheless, as a result of English propaganda, the hidden decisions of high-level financial interests, and the messianic dreams of world peace harbored by President Woodrow Wilson, the United States ultimately entered the war.

After World War I, however, a wave of unfavorable reaction set in among the American public, and the United States pulled back from involvement with European powers. The ugly truth about Britain's manipulation of America came out in a series of studies,[45] and the boom of the 1920s and the depression of the 1930s served to keep Americans concerned with their own affairs.

---

45 Harry Elmer Barnes, *The Genesis of the World War* (New York, N.Y.: Alfred A. Knopf, 1926).
Charles Callan Tansill, *America Goes to War* (Boston, Mass.: Little, Brown, [2nd ed.] 1963).
Walter Millis, *Road To War: America 1914-1917* (New York, N.Y.:

By contrast, in my opinion, America's entrance into World War II had a sound moral justification. In spite of all the ins and outs that historians will continue discussing and sorting through, the fact remains that National Socialism constituted a modern Turk seeking to destroy Christendom. Toward the end of the 19th century and on into the 20th, German life was corrupted heavily by occultism. Spiritualist lodges were everywhere, and liberal theology (Baalism) was taught in schools and pulpits all over the land. The rise to power of National Socialism, with its philosophy of race, blood, power, and the will, was nothing more than an institutionalization of pure pagan occultism and Eastern mysticism.[46] The Church was attacked and silenced, and a campaign of terror was mounted against neighboring nations. It was a time for Christian nations (or at least semi-Christian ones) to band together to remove the menace, and they did so.

After World War II, the United States did not return to her isolationist position. Instead, she was persuaded to head up an amorphous company of Western nations dedicated to "containing" the modern Turk of Russian (and later Chinese) communism.[47] We take up the problem of containment later in this essay. Suffice it here to say that the United States assumed the same stance that Britain formerly did: maintaining a balance of power. After the presidency of Richard Nixon, American foreign policy doctrine sought to play the Soviet Union against Red China—a dangerous, manipulative, and unnecessary game.

Houghton Mifflin Co., 1935).

46 George L. Mosse, "The Mystical Origins of National Socialism," *Journal of the History of Ideas 22* (1961): 81-96.

47 The theory of containment was first set forth in the July, 1947, issue of *Foreign Affairs* by George F. Kennan, writing as "Mr. X." The essay was entitled, "The Sources of Soviet Conduct."

From a Christian standpoint, the involvement of the United States in imperial colonialism was wrong, as was its involvement in wars that were none of its business. The historic policy of the United States had been largely to "mind our own business," and departures from that policy resulted in problems and disasters (such as the Vietnam War). Total isolationism is not the Christian position, but neither is offensive meddling.

THE COLD WAR

When the Union of Soviet Socialist Republics came into being in 1917, its leaders announced their intention to conquer every nation on the earth. They specifically declared the Christian nations of the earth to be their enemies. The Soviet Union never changed this declaration of war and reiterated it many times. The goal of its foreign policy was the domination of the entire world.

Secular liberal humanists would not believe that the Soviet Union really meant what it said, because liberals believe that man is basically good, nice, and peaceful. If the Soviets announced that they were going to "bury" the West, that was just a temper tantrum. ("See, he's pounding with his shoe!") Now, this leftist-liberal mythology suffered a setback each time the Soviet Bear put forth his paw, as he did in the conquest of Eastern Europe after the Second World War, the invasion of Hungary in 1956, the invasion of Czechoslovakia in 1968, the (attempted) conquest of Afghanistan, and so forth. After a few months, however, the liberal religious belief in the goodness of man would surface again, and we were assured that the Soviets really meant well and would not do it again.

It is important to understand that the root problem here is the liberal view of human nature. While evil conspiracies do exist, they are not the major problem.[48] Liberals simply cannot believe that some people are worse than others and that unregenerate human nature is fundamentally evil. Thus, they always moved away from taking various evil rulers' pronouncements seriously and generally tended to assume that such men do not really mean what they say. From a Christian standpoint, this is insanity, a lack of adjustment to reality.

The Soviet declaration of international war should have been taken seriously. That does not mean the West had to invade Russia, but it does mean they needed to take steps to defend themselves.

America was, in a very real sense, at war, and needed to act accordingly. American policy, however, was based on liberal assumptions. American policy since World War II sought the "containment" of the Soviet Union. The idea was to contain the spread of communism. The method was to resist communist advances without ever striking back at aggressors, and to assist friendly nations by means of foreign aid. We take up foreign aid in the next section of this essay. Here we must ask how well this policy of containment worked.

Clearly, containment did not work. During the years that containment was American policy, one nation after another was either subverted or conquered. The reason for this is that the United States, and its allies under its pressure, all too often ignored the biblical rules of war. We saw six of these in Chapter 5:

- Defense, not aggression.
- Assassination of warmongering leadership.

---

[48] Gary North, *Conspiracy: A Biblical View* (Tyler, Tex.: Dominion Press, 1986).

- Negotiation is always an option.
- Protect civilians, fight warmongers.
- Everyone should help defend his nation.
- Local people should deal with the local situation.

To these we can now add a seventh: retaliation. This is implied, as we saw in Chapter 5, from Deut. 20:10ff. If we are attacked by an aggressor, it is not enough to drive the enemy from our soil. We must pursue him to his citadel and teach him a lesson so that he will not come again. The purpose of war is to settle matters that have not been settled by negotiation. War must continue until matters are genuinely settled.

The First Gulf War conducted by the West against Iraq is a case in point. The failure to remove Saddam Hussein from power left continuing problems unresolved in that area. Whether this war was right or wrong from a Christian standpoint, it was poorly conducted as regards the rule of retaliation.

Retaliation is not annihilation, of course, but retaliation is designed to *break the will* of the warmongering nation. As Deut. 20:11 says, "And if it [the enemy city] agrees to make peace with you and opens to you, then all the people who are found in it shall become your forced labor and serve you" (NASB). Now, in the New Covenant we don't expect such tribute to be rendered permanently, but it should be extracted for a long enough period of time to make sure that the warmongering nation is retrained in a more peaceful and righteous direction. I suggest a Jubilee period of 50 years, after which the land would revert to its original national owners. During those fifty years, free trade and open missionary activity would be the rule.

While we are on this point, let me give two illustrations of this principle. The first is the aftermath of the American War Between the States. After that war, the victorious

Northern states reduced the South to the status of a colony, which meant they were forced to buy and sell in terms of Northern desires. This policy kept the South in a poor economic condition and of course exploited poor blacks to the greatest hardship, but it did in time break the "rebel will" of Southern leadership. During this time, the South was dominated largely by Yankee culture because education and the media were largely in Northern hands—this was "missionary work." The New South, arising 100 years later, resembled Yankee culture more than it did the pre-Civil War Southern aristocracy. Whether this cultural shift was good, bad, or a mixture is not at issue. The point is that some kind of "reconstruction" after victory in war is a sound policy.

The second illustration is Germany after World War I. During the period 1918 to 1933, the allies exacted tribute from the losers, but there were no missionaries, and there was no rebuilding. Unlike the Confederate States, which had a common language and some common culture with the Yankees, the Germans were isolated and impoverished. They turned inward and were not "reconstructed."

To return to our earlier point about containment, the basic rule of containment was that they can attack us and our allies, but we never cross their boundaries to retaliate. North Vietnam could invade South Vietnam all it wanted, but America would not invade the North. America did not send in an assassination team to take out Ho Chi Minh; instead America fought for years, killing 14-year-old boys conscripted into the army of North Vietnam, while Uncle Ho slept safe and sound. Some compassionate policy.

Another aspect of containment was conspiratorial activity on the part of the American Central Intelligence Agency. Who knows how much or how little the CIA has really done? I certainly don't. All the same, in times of peace, it is not the place of the United States to meddle in the internal affairs of other states, to destabilize regimes, to support one corrupt government over against another, or to subvert unfriendly governments. Such hidden manipulations in peacetime are the foreign policy of a pagan nation, not a Christian one. Let the United States protect Christian missionaries and free trade. That will do more to fight communism or Islam than any manipulation of regimes can ever do.

Yet a third aspect of containment has been the positioning of American soldiers overseas. While there is a place for a Christian nation to assist its weaker allies, American presence has gone way beyond that. In fact, many nations have failed to develop adequate systems of self-defense precisely because they are counting on the United States to defend them. This is an unhealthy situation and violates the sixth rule of war as we have listed it: Local people should defend their local situation.

FOREIGN AID

One other aspect of American War policy has been foreign aid. The fact is that the foreign policy of the United States has been increasingly messianic. Its goal is to save the world. We have forgotten that only Jesus Christ can save the world. If the world rejects Him, then it will suffer His wrath, and there is nothing we can do about it.

Many parts of the world are suffering intensely today. There are reasons for this. One significant factor emerges from the fact that during the 19th and early 20th centuries, Christian missions took the gospel of Jesus Christ to all the nations of the earth. The message may have been somewhat obscured by colonialism and imperialism, but the Bible assures us that Truth is Truth, and men cannot help but hear the Truth when it is proclaimed. They may hear it and bow the knee, or they may hear it and reject it. But they do hear it.

Today, the nations that heard the Truth and rejected it are suffering under the wrath of God (Deut. 28:15-68). They are suffering famine, starvation, deportation, wars, disease, and oppression. Christian people should and do help alleviate this suffering as best we can, but Christians dare not be naive about it. Until men repent, they will continue to live in the earthly down-payment of hell.

Secular humanists do not believe these truths, however. They believe in *salvation by money*. They also believe in *salvation by the state*. Put these together and what do you get? Foreign aid: money given from one state to another for the purpose of buying salvation. Since the Second World War, the United States government has given hundreds of billions of dollars in foreign aid to other governments. Did it stop the march of communism? Clearly not. The march of communism stopped only because of rot from within the Soviet Union.

David Chilton has summarized the three most important and obvious effects of the American foreign aid giveaway program.

> "First, *foreign aid produces irresponsibility and dependence*. Capital is turned over to be spent by people who do not bear the cost. This creates waste. If you are spending your own money, you have an incentive to be careful, and to make sure that it is invested in productive, profitable enterprises. The executive with an unlimited expense account will be tempted to eat lavish dinners with the company money. He will use his own funds to save toward a new set of tires."[49]

---

49 David Chilton, *Productive Christians in an Age of Guilt Manipulators*, third edition (Tyler, Tex.: Institute for Chris- tian Economics, 1985), 107. Chilton draws heavily upon the research of P. T. Bauer, presented in his *Dissent on Development* (Cambridge, Mass.: Harvard University

Second, writes Chilton, "*foreign aid helps those who are better off, rather than the poor.*"[50] After all, who receives the foreign aid? The ruling elite of the foreign country, and in most cases that means the strongman who got to the top by crushing everyone else will benefit from foreign aid. Foreign aid is paid by governments to governments—that is, by rulers to rulers. The people seldom see any of it.

"Third, *foreign aid actually widens the gap between rich and poor nations,*" Chilton writes, adding that "it inhibits those factors that would produce growth (e.g., by creating dependence rather than responsibility). More than this, it encourages explicit envy toward the rich, who are held to be responsible for the plight of those below them."[51]

It may be objected, however, that the Marshall Plan did help rebuild Europe and for a time at least created much good will. That is true because the Marshall Plan was administered better than modern foreign aid programs and because the receiving nations were governed by good men, not savage strongmen like so many in the "third world" nations that today get foreign aid. All the same, the Marshall Plan would have been much more efficient if it had consisted of tax breaks for American industry rather than simply grants of tax money to foreign nations. American businessmen could have been given a ten-year tax break as an incentive to invest in Europe. This would have done more to develop local economies and would have been much cheaper all around.

There is no biblical justification for the U.S. government taxing its citizenry and then sending the money to support governmental officials in other nations. True financial assistance to people in distress should come through the

---

Press, 1976), and his *Reality and Rhetoric: Studies in the Economics of Development* (Cambridge, Mass.: Harvard, 1984).

50 Ibid., 108.

51 Ibid., 109.

One True International Organization: the Church of Jesus Christ. Long-term economic development should come through free trade. These will be our themes in Chapter 12.

International Communications

I will ask the Father, and He will give you another Helper, so that He may be with you forever; the Helper is the Spirit of truth, whom the world cannot receive, because it does not see Him or know Him; but you know Him because He remains with you and will be in you.
— John 14:16-17 (New American Standard Version)

Human beings are created in the image of God. This means that man is to image, at a "secondary" or created level, the life of God. Now, we can say that God is a Holy Society, consisting of three Persons. These persons are in constant personal fellowship, face to face. Similarly, human relationships at their best are face-to-face relationships.

It is important for men to have personal relationships with the three Persons of God. God chooses to meet with us face-to-face. As we get to know God better, we grow in confidence and faith. On the other hand, if our prayer life slackens, we begin to mistrust God and become fearful and afraid.

The same principle applies in human life. We tend to be more suspicious of people we don't know than of people we do know. Personal *presence* is important, and in this section, we want to discuss the relevance of this fact for international relations.

PERSONAL CONTACT

How often in life do we find misunderstandings arise simply because of problems of communication, in marriage for instance? This problem is often magnified on the international level because of differences of language. An advertising campaign for an American cat food stressed that their product would provide nourishment for all nine of your cat's lives. When this advertising campaign was translated and used in another country, however, it became the source of all kinds of jokes, because in that country cats only have seven lives. Similarly, plans to advertise the Chevrolet Nova automobile in Spanish-speaking countries had to be scrapped when it was realized that *no va* means "doesn't go."

Because they believe human nature is basically good, secular humanists tend to reduce *all* international problems to matters of communication requiring "negotiation." Thus, the humanist agenda stresses conferences, colloquies, symposia, meetings, shuttle diplomacy, international forums, and so forth. If people only learn to understand one another, they believe, then people will get along. After all, communist leaders only want for their people the same good things we want for ours.

From a Christian point of view, such thinking is stupid and naive. Jesus minced no words about human goodness: "So if you, despite being evil..." (Matt. 7:11)—such was His assessment of human nature. Moreover, while all sin is equally offensive to the holiness and majesty of God, some sin is worse than others, and some men are more evil than others (1 John 5:16).

In discussing what makes some sins worse than others, the Presbyterian *Westminster Larger Catechism*—produced one hundred years after the Reformation and summarizing universal Christian belief on this point—states that sins are aggravated in four ways: First, from the person who commits the sin, if he is older, holds a high office, is in a position of leadership, etc. Second, from the parties offended, if against God Himself, or persons representing Him, or the poor, or many persons at once, etc. Third, from the nature of the offense, if it scandalizes many people, cannot be rectified, is committed after warnings, if repeated, etc. And fourth, from circumstances of time and place, if during worship, in public, etc.[52]

Just as some persons are worse than others, so some nations are worse than others. God told Abraham that He would give him the whole land of Canaan, but not for four hundred and thirty years because "the wrongdoing of the Amorite is not yet complete" (Gen. 15:16, NASB). These nations were not yet so consumed with evil that God would have to liquidate them totally. Eventually, they would get to that point, just as the whole world had before the Flood (Gen. 6:5-7).

Some nations are Christian, and some are not. Some heathen nations are worse than others. Some Christian nations are relatively more sanctified than others, just as some Christian churches are better than others (for proof, read Revelation 2 and 3). These facts must be taken into account in international relations.

At the same time, the liberal humanist perspective does contain a kernel of truth, however distorted. Communication can be a problem in a multi-language,

---

52 See *Westminster Larger Catechism*, questions 150 and 151.

multi-cultural world. For that reason, the Christian nation should have open communications with the other nations of the world, but the Christian nation should not be naive about human nature.

UNDERSTANDING

In order to facilitate such communication and understanding, the secular humanist turns to politics. We need lots of embassies, consulates, international meetings, Peace Corps workers, and the like, they say. While the Christian position does not totally eliminate all such political contacts, our emphasis lies elsewhere.

A Christian foreign policy is anchored by Church relations, missions, and free trade. Think about it for a minute: Who gets to know a foreign people better: an ambassador secluded in an embassy, or a merchant engaged in continual business dealings with a foreign company? Politicians who deal only with other politicians, or a missionary who deals with people day by day? The answers are obvious.

Why should American tax money be spent to maintain a huge company of politicians and bureaucrats in foreign nations? A mere token presence for emergencies could suffice. When trouble arises, our government should consult with missionaries and merchants in order to gain a better understanding of the other country. Such a practice would not only alleviate the tax burden on the American people, it would get us better information.

The reality is that most of the countries of the world are ruled by strongmen who came to power by stomping on the faces of other people. International *political* relations are relations among such strongmen, and such strongmen tend to unite with each other *against the people*. Note the alliance between Ahab and Ben-Hadad (1 Kings 20), or between Pilate and Herod (Luke 23:12). International *political* relations create a very distorted view of the world as a result. The Christian faith has a creative alternative to such dealings.

SPIES AND INFORMANTS

When another country manifests pronounced and prolonged hostility toward our nation, it is a good thing for us to get information about them and their plans. This means we need spies and informants. Good intelligence can enable the Christian nation to do things that make for peace by heading off conflicts, thus saving lives.

Is such spying legitimate? Certainly, if it makes for peace. We are all familiar with the spies who went into Jericho and checked out the situation before Joshua attacked that city (Joshua 2). Earlier, Moses had sent spies into Canaan to look over the land and find its weak points. Unfortunately, the faithless and cowardly spies only saw its strongholds. (See Numbers 13 and 14.) This was a special situation, though. It was the conquest of the land God had given Israel. A story with perhaps more relevance is found in 2 Kings 6:

> Now the king of Aram was making war against Israel; and he consulted with his servants, saying, "In such and such a place shall be my camp." But the man of God sent word to the king of Israel, saying, "Be careful that you do not pass this place, because the Arameans are coming down there." And the king of Israel sent scouts to the place about which the man of God had told him; so he warned him, so that he was on his guard there, more than once or twice. Now the heart of the king of Aram was enraged over this matter; and he called his servants and said to them, "Will you not tell me which of us is for the

> king of Israel?" One of his servants said, "No, my lord,
> the king; but Elisha, the prophet who is in Israel, tells the
> king of Israel the words that you speak in your bedroom."
> (2 Kings 6:8-12, NASB)

Seemingly this was a miraculous event. Elisha was getting information from angelic informants or from the Holy Spirit. All the same, it shows the moral validity of spying: If angels or the Spirit can do it in times of "cold war," then so can Christian spies.

But was it a miracle? In the preceding chapter, we have the story of Naaman the *Syrian*. One of his servant girls was an Israelite, and Naaman himself was converted after Elisha cleansed his leprosy (1 Kings 5). Is it possible that Naaman, the Syrian commander, was slipping information to Elisha via a network of Syrian believers? Is it possible that it was Naaman who told the king of Syria that Elisha had "miraculous access" to their war plans in order to divert suspicion from himself?

The purpose is peace, and the Christian nation is to be a peaceful nation as much as possible. If war can be averted by good intelligence, then let it be averted.

PSYCHOLOGICAL OPERATIONS

When Jesus ascended on high, He sent His Holy Spirit to work on the hearts of men. This was the beginning of God's great psychological warfare against wickedness. The great tools of psychological warfare are *propaganda* and *kindness*. The great American expert on psy-war was a devout Christian named Paul M. L. Linebarger. In his book, *Psychological Warfare*, Linebarger states that "...in the narrow sense, psychological warfare comprises the use of propaganda against an enemy, together with such military operational measures as may supplement the propaganda. Propaganda may be described, in turn, as organized persuasion by non-violent means."[53] We are used to thinking of "propaganda" in negative terms, but the saturation of a community with the gospel of truth is, from one point of view, great propaganda and psychological warfare.

When the king of Syria realized that Elisha was telling the king of Israel all his plans, he set out to capture Elisha. God protected the prophet and struck the Syrians with a form of mental blindness that caused them not to realize who Elisha was.[54] Elisha led them to the capital of Northern Israel, Samaria:

> When they had come into Samaria, Elisha said, "Lord, open the eyes of these men, so that they may see." So the Lord opened their eyes, and they saw; and behold, they were in the midst of Samaria. Then the king of Israel when he saw them, said to Elisha, "My father, shall I kill them? Shall I kill them?" (2 Kings 6:20-21, NASB)

Notice Elisha's answer and its effect:

> But he answered, "You shall not kill them. Would you kill those whom you have taken captive with your sword and your bow? Set bread and water before them, so that they may eat and drink, and go to their master." So he provided a large feast for them; and when they had eaten and drunk, he sent them away, and they went to their master. And the marauding bands of Arameans did not come again into the land of Israel. (2 Kings 6:22-23, NASB)

---

53 Paul M. L. Linebarger, *Psychological Warfare* (New York, N.Y.: Duell, Sloan and Pierce, 1954), 25.
Linebarger's book and the science fiction stories he published under the pen-name "Cordwainer Smith" are a gold mine of ideas regarding psychological warfare.

54 The Hebrew word translated "blindness" here only occurs one other time in the Bible, in Gen. 19:11.
It is not the regular word for blindness. In both cases, it would be better translated "confusion" or "bedazzlement." Actual blindness is clearly not what happened in either case. Perhaps they experienced migraines.

The *kindness* shown to these men took all the fight out of them—at least temporarily, for they did return to make war on Israel again a few years later (2 Kings 6:24ff.).

There are a couple of qualifiers to note. First, kindness is shown to ordinary soldiers, not to warmongers. In 1 Kings 20, Ahab was cursed by God because he showed mercy to the evil king of Syria who had made war against Israel repeatedly and had blasphemed the Lord (cf. 1 Kings 20:31, 42). Second, the specific kindness of serving a meal has an additional overtone in the Bible, that of inviting these men to convert to the faith. Israel was to be a priest to the nations, feeding them the Word of God, which is always symbolized by a meal in the Bible (as in the Lord's Supper today). Similarly, if a Christian nation shows kindness to captured troops of an enemy, it should always be in such a way as to show forth the Truth of the gospel.

After World War I, the allied nations exacted retribution from the German people and thereby needlessly aggravated post-war relations. The result was the rise to power of the National Socialist party under Adolf Hitler. Happily, wiser heads prevailed after World War II, and the Marshall Plan and MacArthur's policies of kindness helped Germany and Japan to rebuild, making them into strong allies of the United States. (We looked in Chapter 7 at whether the Marshall Plan was the best way to accomplish this goal.)

Truth and charity, propaganda and kindness, are the primary weapons in the Christian's arsenal. They find their most important use in the missionary task of the Church, but they are of value in international relations as well.

INTERNATIONAL FORUMS

While secular humanists make too much of international forums for discussion, some Christian conservatives make too little of them. We look at this in more depth in Chapter

9, but we should make a couple of observations about it here.

The primary international forum should be in the Church. A model we can look at is the Vatican. (As a Protestant, I have a lot of problems with the Vatican, of course; but the notion of an international forum for discussion is not unique to Roman Catholicism.) The great Councils held by the Vatican enable bishops from all countries of the world to come together to discuss the problems the faith is encountering—all sorts of problems, social as well as theological. Though such Councils are not often held, international discussion is continuous at the Vatican. Similarly, the Eastern churches get together for discussion at Ecumenical Synods. And of course, there is the World Council of Churches. While the *content* of such meetings is frequently deplorable (usually little more than baptized humanism), the *idea* of such international Church meetings is entirely proper. We see the first one in Acts 15, after all.

Similarly, a place set aside for representatives of Christian nations to meet is not a bad idea. In centuries past, the court of the Holy Roman Emperor provided such a forum, a place where problems could be talked out and the wisdom of skilled mediators tapped. In a secular, pagan world such as ours, this sounds like a fabulous dream, but if God brings revival, who knows?

CONCLUSION

The God in whose image we are made is a Person, in fact, three Persons. Each Person has perfect communication with the others, and God seeks to have such communication with His children. Applying this truth to international affairs, we find that, as in all of life, face-to-face communications can often alleviate problems before they become too intense, thus making for peace. Christians dare not be naive about this, though, because we know that many men are evil and have evil desires that cannot be placated by negotiation.

For the Christian, the primary ways to achieve international understanding are through the Church, free trade, and the open exchange of knowledge and the arts, not through the work of politicians. In working to create such a positive environment for communication, Christian nations should engage in serious "psychological warfare" using propaganda (the Truth) and kindness, in order to prevent the outbreak of hostilities.

The United Nations

The kings of the earth take their stand
And the rulers conspire together
Against Yahweh and against His Anointed, saying,
"Let's tear their shackles apart
And throw their ropes away from us!"
He who sits in the heavens laughs,
Yahweh scoffs at them.

— Psalm 2:2-3 (New American Standard Bible)

The United Nations figured very prominently in American foreign policy during the presidency of George Bush, and thus it remains an important factor in world affairs. The United Nations embodies the pagan, Babelic concept of political salvation and continues to inspire the hopes of secular humanists. Thus, whether the U.N. maintains its position in global politics or dwindles in importance, we should take some time to reflect on what it means for us.

TRUE INTERNATIONALISM

Before considering the false Babelic internationalism represented by the U.N., let us review the elements of true Christian internationalism. In a little-known but very important essay, Rousas J. Rushdoony has called attention to the difference between Christian and pagan internationalism. His remarks summarize the position we have been discussing in this book and are worth quoting at length.

Rushdoony states that the 19th century was an era of genuine internationalism. Summarizing his argument, he writes:

> True internationalism rests not on ideas of world unity through worldwide political coercion, but on a free order wherein men, ideas, and goods can move freely across borders in terms of the liberty of all.
>
> Because the nineteenth century was more or less firmly committed to a hard money policy, to gold and silver, an internationalism of trade and travel prevailed. Transportation facilities were steadily extended throughout Europe, the Americas, Africa, and Asia, and trade penetrated the far corners of the world. Traders might have strongly nationalistic and racial ideas, but free trade and hard money were color blind and knew no frontiers. Men and goods travelled freely across boundaries to a degree unknown to the mid-twentieth century, and ideas followed them everywhere.
>
> The nineteenth century was also the great era of missionary expansion by evangelical Christianity, an internationalistic faith holding to the salvation of all manners, classes, and colors of men in the true Church of Jesus Christ, and congregations prayed for the conversion of the heathen and received with joy the missionary reports of the regeneration of previously depraved savages and idolators....[Congregations sang missionary hymns] in Sunday School or church as a missionary offering was received, and thousands upon thousands went out as missionaries in a day when being a missionary spelled sacrifice, hardship, sickness, and death, because they were moved by a Christian internationalism, by a desire to

bring the unregenerate into salvation and into Christian civilization. Schools and hospitals were established by the missionaries, and outstanding converts were sent to the homeland to be trained in theology and in terms of Christian civilization in order to reproduce it in Africa, Asia, and the Pacific Islands.

This was internationalism, and this powerful movement, combined with political and economic liberty, made the nineteenth the century of internationalism. Men looked beyond their own frontiers, were moved by a sense of Christian responsibility for the eternal and material welfare of others, and a genuine internationalism flourished. This internationalism did not dream of an organic union of nations and a political order: It did visualize a Christian world and free political orders and world-wide free economics.

Meanwhile, however, other forces were working for precisely this organic internationalism and world state. From the French Revolution on, international socialism, and later Marxist and non-Marxist socialism, began to work for a world of unity in terms of statist equality, usually an equality gained by the extermination of all classes save one, the intellectually defined 'workers' class. This internationalism has no sense of 'brotherhood' beyond its ideologically defined boundaries: It hates with passion all who are outside the socialist camp, and it often hates and kills its own socialist brethren. In terms of this new 'internationalism,' the borders began to close tightly, and the old free world began to resolve itself into a series of prison camps called socialist and welfare states.[55]

---

55 Rousas J. Rushdoony, "Has the U.N. Replaced Christ as a World Religion?" in Kenneth W. Ingwalson, *Your Church—Their Target* (Arlington, Va.: Better Books, 1966), 215-218.

Rushdoony points to the internationalism of free trade and world missions that operated during the 19th century, but behind that flowering of international concern there was a centuries-old Christian tradition. Christopher Dawson summarizes that heritage:

> It is true that in the New Testament the emphasis is rather on the breaking down of national barriers and the universality of the Gospel—that "God has made of one blood all nations of men that dwell on the face of the earth"—and that in Christ there is "neither Jew nor Greek, neither bond nor free, neither male nor female." It was only in the Church that this ultimate fact of the unity and brotherhood of the human race was realized and expressed. The Christians were "a chosen race, a royal priesthood, a holy nation, a people for God's own possession."[56]

At the cultural level, of course, each nation is to glorify God in its own unique ways, but undergirding all these nations is the universal body of Christ manifest in the Church:

> The history of Christendom is the history of a culture based on this idea of spiritual universalism—which was more than an idea, because it was embodied in the super-political society of the Church. With the conversion, first of the Roman Empire and then of the barbarians, there was formed a community of peoples sharing a common spiritual tradition which was transmitted from age to age and from people to people until it embraced the whole of Europe. More than this, it created Europe. For the European continent is the result of the European culture and not vice versa. From the physical point of view Europe is not a unity but simply the north western extension of the Asiatic land mass. Nor is it a racial unity, for from prehistoric times it has been a melting pot of races and a meeting ground of cultural traditions of the most diverse

---

56 Christopher Dawson, *The Judgment of the Nations* (New York, N.Y.: Sheed and Ward, 1942), 203-204.

> origin. The formal principle of European unity is not physical but spiritual. Europe was Christendom: It was the society of Christian peoples which for a thousand years, more or less, had been molded by the same religious and intellectual influence until it possessed a consciousness of spiritual community which transcended political and racial limits. As long as this spiritual community was recognized as a concrete social reality...the political unit held a relatively humble place.[57]

Throughout the Christian centuries, the European nations shared a common outlook and saw themselves as part of one larger society, Christendom. There was no "one-world state," but there was plenty of cooperation, particularly in repelling the common foe. It is hard for us to understand the kinds of cooperation that were common in the Christian centuries, because society was more complex then. A society that is growing and flowering on the basis of the Oneness and Threeness of God is a society with many rich and complex aspects. Our modern society is much simplified by comparison: Humanism shaves off anything that cannot be grasped and controlled by the human mind.

Let us take one example of the kind of Christian internationalism in earlier times, the so-called Knights of Malta. During the Middle Ages, when Jerusalem was a center of Christian pilgrimage, there were always hospitals there to help the pilgrims. During the 1000s, one of these was restored and dedicated to St. John the Baptist. The company of men maintaining the hospital were known as the Order of St. John. After the Crusaders took Jerusalem, many Christian warriors sought to join the fraternity, and a regular religious order was established. In 1118, the monastic knights took an oath to become militant defenders of the cause of the Cross. During the 1100s, the Knights of the Order of the Hospital of St. John of Jerusalem, as

---

57 Ibid., 204-205.

they came to be called, took an increasingly active role in fighting the Moslems, but they always kept their hospital work first and foremost.

By the 1300s, the Knights of St. John, or Knights Hospitallers, had chapters all over Europe, organized in eight groups or divisions: those of Provence, Auvergne, France, Italy, Aragon, Spain, England, and Germany. The chapters were largely occupied with the building, furnishing, and improving of hospitals, especially along pilgrim routes, to which were attached learned physicians and surgeons who had the privilege of eating with the Knights. The military branch protected pilgrims, guarded the hospitals, and defended Christendom from the Moslems.

Around 1300, the European presence in the Holy Land had lost out to the Moslems, and the Knights of St. John moved their headquarters to the island of Rhodes. From that base they acted to protect Europe. They became a naval power, maintained a fleet of galleys, and for two centuries harassed pirates, Moslem troublemakers, and Turks. Their consuls in Egypt and Jerusalem watched over the interests of pilgrims. And they kept up their hospitals.

So skilled were the Knights of St. John in fighting Islamic invaders that important efforts were made to drive them from their base at Rhodes. In 1440 and 1444, they repelled attacks from Egypt. In 1480, they held at bay an Ottoman fleet and army. A still greater attack was mounted in 1522 by Suleiman the Magnificent. Reinforcements failed, the Christian powers sent no assistance, and in the next year the Knights capitulated, withdrawing to Crete. Their occupation of Rhodes had postponed for about two centuries the appearance of the Ottomans as a first-rate naval power in the Mediterranean, a debt that Europe never sufficiently acknowledged.

The emperor Charles V granted the island of Malta to the Knights, and this is why they became known popularly as the Knights of Malta. From this base, they continued to be a stumbling block for Turkish designs on Europe, scoring a significant victory in 1550. Determined to wipe out this international order of Christian Knights once and for all, the Ottoman fleet appeared off the island on May 18, 1565, and one of the most famous sieges in history began. The Turkish invasion concluded, in failure, in September after the appearance of a large relieving force sent by the Spanish viceroy of Sicily, *after the Knights had killed 25,000 of the enemy.*

In the years that followed, because of the Reformation, the Knights dwindled in importance. In recent years, however, the Knights of Malta have resumed their hospital work. There are at least three branches: the Roman Catholic branch, a German Lutheran branch, and a Protestant branch centered in England (the St. John Ambulance Association and the St. John Ambulance Brigade). Though no longer one unified order, and no longer a military force, the Knights of Malta still exist to serve Christendom.[58] As Bradford has written:

> The battlefield is now the world. The Order's activities range from centers for the treatment and rehabilitation of lepers in Africa, South America, and Polynesia, to ambulance units in Ireland and Germany, hospitals and research clinics, and field units which are flown to any disaster area. All the more remarkable in the second half of the twentieth century is the fact that all this is personal, and privately financed.[59]

---

58 *Encyclopaedia Britannica*, Ninth Edition: Vol. 21, 173-175; 1954 Edition: Vol. 19, 836-838. Most important reading in this area is Ernle Bradford, *The Shield and the Sword: The Knights of St. John, Jerusalem, Rhodes, and Malta* (New York, N.Y.: E. P. Dutton, 1973).

59 Bradford, *The Shield and the Sword*, 223.

The story of the Knights of St. John makes an important point: It is possible and reasonable for a company of Christian nations to permit, cooperate with, and maintain an elite guard against a common foe. While the Bible teaches that the sword is given only to civil magistrates, here we have a small army maintained by a loose confederation of such magistrates, commissioned to perform a specific task.

BABELIC INTERNATIONALISM

As Dawson sees it, modern secular humanism is trying to keep a sense of European and Western unity, but without the Christian faith. Even more, modern pagan man wants total world unity without Christianity. Dawson's book concerns the failure of the League of Nations, and his fundamental insight is:

> ...the League of Nations was, in fact, from the beginning nothing else but a league of States, and membership of the League was based entirely on the fact of political sovereignty without any reference to the national character of the societies in question.[60]

This is no small matter. As we have seen, a nation is a very different thing from a temporary political order. As Dawson puts it:

> ...the Nations are permanent factors which remain whether they are given juridical recognition or not; whereas States, as we have only too much reason to realize of late years, can change their form and be multiplied or diminished by wars and revolutions with or without justice or the will of the peoples concerned. A period like that of the Napoleonic Wars witnesses a

---

60 Dawson, *Judgment of the Nations*, 79

> wholesale massacre of States, some of which disappeared for ever, while others reappeared in a new form when the storm had passed.[61]

Dawson notes that the League of Nations broke down because there was no undergirding belief sustaining it. No one wanted a *Christian* League. As a result, the European countries sought unity on another basis. One solution was to create unity by force based on the Aryan race, and the other was to create unity by forcing all the world into one controlled economy, called communism. Commenting on National Socialism, Dawson writes:

> Thus, the racialist ideology, like the Communist ideology, is a result of the breakdown of European unity and of the attempt to find a substitute for it in some primary social element which is permanent and indestructible. But if, as we believe, Europe was essentially a spiritual unity, based on religion and expressed in culture, it cannot be replaced by a biological [Nazism] or economic [Communism] unit, because these belong to a different plane of social reality. They are social elements, not social organisms in the full sense.[62]

The United Nations was founded as an international secular church with salvation as its explicit goal. The Preamble to its Charter declares, "We the peoples of the United Nations determined to *save* succeeding generation from the scourge of war...." Rushdoony comments, "The U.N. is thus 'determined to save'; it is thus possessed with all the sense of inevitability and missionary fervor that any religious groups possesses."[63]

---

61 Idem.

62 Ibid., 210.

63 Rousas J. Rushdoony, "The United Nations," in *The Nature of the American System* (Fairfax, Va.: Thoburn Press [1965] 1978), 116.

Rushdoony has described the salvation-goal of the U.N. as direct opposition to Christianity: "The U.N. holds as its basic premise a thesis which has a long history in both religion and in politics, the doctrine of *salvation by law*."[64] Analyzing numerous U.N. statements and the writings of its proponents, Rushdoony summarizes:

> Two aspects of this premise have already become manifest: First, that the hope and salvation of man and of society is through world law, and, second, that the essence or at least the primary factor in peace is environmental rather than personal.[65]

The U.N. denies that war arises from "the lusts that war in your members" (James 4:1). Instead, the founders and followers of the U.N. insist that war arises from social inequalities. World law is needed, they say, to destroy such inequalities and thus eliminate war.

But what law? They do not want biblical or Christian law—the foundation of true social peace. They want a common morality that arises from the human consciousness.

Rushdoony comments that the basic assumption of the U.N. is:

> ...the rule of law is the rule of morality, which is faith in man.... The world problem again appears, in this focus, not as a need for regeneration but for reorganization, not a change in man's nature but a change in man's legal and institutional environment.[66]

Thus:

> ...it is denied that economics or religion are separate law spheres; both are subordinate to politics, to world politics,

---

64 Ibid., 114.

65 Ibid., 115.

66 Ibid., 121f.

which must govern to secure "conditions or economic and social progress and development." Religious differences are denied any validity, for no distinction as to religion is permitted.[67]

Rushdoony insists that the United Nations can never achieve its goal:

> The U.N. believes in salvation by law, but in no historic sense does it have law. The two central definitions of law are (1) the binding custom or practice of a community, or (2) the commandments or revelations of God.... Law, however, can also be the rule of conduct and action *prescribed by a supreme governing authority and enforced thereby*. Such law from early times has been called tyranny.[68]

Law cannot save men; only Jesus Christ can. Salvation by law means tyranny.

In a third powerful essay, Rushdoony shows that the United Nations must claim the attributes of God Himself in order to carry out its aims. "The first and basic requirement of a theology is the unity of the godhead."[69] In order to unify humanity, U.N. dreamers have schemed to shuffle populations of people all over the world, mixing them up, *in order to destroy the God-ordained nations*.[70] This, of course, was the policy of ancient Assyria and Babylon.

Rushdoony goes on to point out that "a second basic requirement of an effective theology is the omnipotence of

---

67　Ibid., 122f.

68　Ibid., 130. Italics added.

69　Rousas J. Rushdoony, "The United Nations: A Religious Dream," in *Politics of Guilt and Pity* (Fairfax, Va.: Thoburn Press, [1970] 1978), 186.

70　Ibid., 186-194.

the godhead." Thus, U.N. dreamers live for the day when their one-world state will have enough power to enforce their plans on everyone.[71]

"A third basic aspect of the godhead is omniscience."[72] Thus, the U.N. commissions tons of reports on every aspect of international life. Moreover, U.N. dreamers seek "to gain this total knowledge of us, first, by controlling our education, second, by controlling our minds through its program of mental health, and, third, by controls invading our privacy."[73]

CONCLUSION

The United Nations does not really *exist*, any more than the "state" *exists*. The U.N. is an assembly of *people*, people committed to playing god. These are the only kind of people attracted to the U.N., and thus the U.N. bureaucracy is filled with people who want to dominate and manipulate other people—power-hungry people who get their jollies from playing god.

As we saw in Chapter 1, however, God always acts to shatter man's Towers of Babel, and the bureaucrats of United Nations are not going to succeed in their dreams. Still, however, their very presence is a continuing threat to Christians worldwide and to the United States in particular. The United Nations is supported largely by American money, since nobody else really believes this garbage. Moreover, the presence of the U.N. on U.S. soil provides a nest for international spies of all sorts.

---

71 Ibid., 194.

72 Ibid., 194.

73 Ibid., 196. A very important case study in the United Nations, and its attempts to play god, is George Grant's interaction with the U.N.'s 1987 Year of the Homeless. See Grant, *The Dispossessed: Homelessness in America* (Westchester, Ill.: Crossway Books, 1986).

In another time, in another era, Christian nations might set up a common meeting place to exchange ideas, discuss concerns, and avert conflicts. We are not living in such a time. The U.N. is nothing but organized, militant paganism. Christians obviously reject the pagan dream of the United Nations as it is stated. Christians must oppose the policies and practices of U.N. representatives as these oppress Christianity worldwide, and American Christians should particularly work to defund the U.N. and have it removed from their borders.

Sanctuary

I will appoint you a place to which he may flee.
— Exod. 21:13 (New American Standard Bible)

The idea of sanctuary is derived from God's presence in His creation. On the one hand, God is everywhere (omnipresent), but at the same time, God makes Himself manifest at certain times and places. We call this God's special presence. In Chapter 8, we took up the principle of personal presence as it pertains to maintaining international peace. In this chapter, we want to note some of the social implications of the fact that God establishes His special presence at certain places.

As we saw in Chapter 5, when God manifests Himself He manifests an environment around Himself called "glory." This glory cloud has a boundary, we observed. Within this boundary, the environment of glory or holiness is God's *sanctuary*. During the Old Covenant, God established one central sanctuary on the earth where His throne was set: first the Tabernacle and later the Temple. At the same time, God told Israel to set up various other kinds of sanctuaries. These were not places where God was specially present, but they were places reserved for special protection. This principle of sanctuary came into the Christian Church, and the Church has always been a sanctuary for those who flee to her for refuge.

The principle of sanctuary is important for international relations for basically three reasons. First, it safeguards the inviolability of the Church and clarifies how the (international) Church acts to disciple the nations (Matthew 28:19). Second, in a Christian land, such as the United States once was, it guarantees the right of free immigration, as we see in Chapter 11. Third, it forms the foundation for such things as embassies and consulates.

THE OLD TESTAMENT SANCTUARY SYSTEM

The fullest description of the sanctuary system in Israel is found in Numbers 35:

> Then Yahweh spoke to Moses, saying, "Speak to the sons of Israel and say to them, 'When you cross the Jordan into the land of Canaan, then you shall select for yourselves cities to be your cities of refuge, so that the one who commits manslaughter by killing a person unintentionally may flee there. The cities shall serve you as a refuge from the avenger, so that the one who commits manslaughter does not die until he stands before the congregation for trial. So the cities which you are to provide shall be six cities of refuge for you. You shall provide three cities across the Jordan, and three cities in the land of Canaan; they are to be cities of refuge. These six cities shall be a refuge for the sons of Israel, for the stranger, and for the foreign resident among them; so that anyone who kills a person unintentionally may flee there. (Num. 35:9-15, NASB)

The ensuing verses describe how the sanctuary functioned. If one man accidentally slew another through carelessness, he could flee to the city of refuge for sanctuary. The next of kin of the slain man was required to track him down and avenge the killing. Once the manslayer arrived at the city of refuge, he was safe.

"Then the congregation shall judge between the one who fatally struck the victim and the blood avenger in accordance with these ordinances" (Num. 35:24, NASB). If the manslayer were guilty of murder, he would be delivered up to death. If he were innocent, he would be protected.

The cities of refuge were held and administered by the Levites, the officers of the Israelite Church (Num. 35:1-13). Thus, the Church acted as a kind of "defense attorney," giving the accused man an opportunity to defend himself before the "congregation" (that is, the elders of the congregation, who sat as judges). The next of kin was required to act as a prosecutor, in that he drove the accused man to the sanctuary and made the charge against him.[74]

In 1 Kings 1, we have a case of this law in operation. When David was old, many of his retainers wanted to make his son Adonijah king, but David proclaimed Solomon king. When this happened, Adonijah became afraid, because he had already presumed royal prerogatives. He fled to a sanctuary, in this case the altar at the Tabernacle:

> Adonijah also was afraid of Solomon, and he got up, and went, and took hold of the horns of the altar. Now it was reported to Solomon, saying, "Behold, Adonijah is afraid of King Solomon, for behold, he has taken hold of the horns of the altar, saying, 'May King Solomon swear to me today that he will not put his servant to death with the sword.'" (1 Kings 1:50-51, NASB)

---

74 See also Deut. 19:1-13. For a fuller discussion of the cities of refuge and how they operated, see Jordan, *The Law of the Covenant*.

By calling himself Solomon's servant, Adonijah was pledging good behavior and submission to Solomon's kingship.

"And Solomon said, 'If he is a worthy man, not one of his hairs will fall to the ground; but if wickedness is found in him, he will die'" (1 Kings 1:52, NASB). This was the judgment passed by the court, in this case by the king himself. "So King Solomon sent men, and they brought him down from the altar. And he came and prostrated himself before King Solomon, and Solomon said to him, 'Go to your house'" (1 Kings 1:53, NASB).

Such was the first and primary function of the sanctuary in Israel: as a place where an accused person could flee and hide until justice could be done. This was not the only form of sanctuary, however.

The entire land of Israel was a sanctuary to people in the nations. Anyone could at any time come into the land and settle as a "stranger or sojourner." They had to settle in the cities, however, because the agricultural land in Israel was under the Jubilee law (Leviticus 25) and reverted to its original owners every fifty years.[75] This excluded foreigners from ever owning land unless they were adopted into an Israelite family. The cities were different, however.

---

75 There are a lot of misunderstandings of the Jubilee law floating around today. The Jubilee was not a land redistribution scheme and has nothing to do with "land reform" of any sort. It was a peculiar law for Israel alone, whereby every fifty years the land reverted to its original owners. Such a law would be extremely unjust in any modern nation because it would automatically disinherit immigrants every fifty years. The purpose of the Jubilee law had to do with Israel's calling to be a peculiar nation of priests. The Land was a larger Sanctuary, and as the Tabernacle space was never to leave the priests, so the Land could never leave Israelites. In Luke 4:18-27, Jesus said that He was bringing the Great Year of Jubilee to the whole world, Gentiles included. The whole world was going to revert to its original owners, the Lord God Almighty and His people, while heathen squatters were going to be converted or disinherited.

Thus, the Jubilee law has been fulfilled. For details on how it operated, read Leviticus 25. For a discussion of modern Jubileeism, see Chilton, *Productive Christians*, 153ff., 257ff.

The fundamental law that expresses this is found in Deut. 23:15-16: "You shall not hand over to his master a slave who has escaped from his master to you. He shall live with you in your midst, in the place that he chooses in one of your towns where it pleases him; you shall not mistreat him" (NASB). This law is not talking about runaway Hebrew slaves, who were indentured for set periods of time either to pay back debts or as punishment for theft (Exod. 21:2; 22:3). The context here is someone who escapes from the nations roundabout Israel (cf. Deut. 23:1-8, 17-20). Any servant (citizen) who leaves his foreign master (ruler) is free to live in any Israelite city he chooses. There was no quota on such immigration. We comment on this aspect of the sanctuary system in Chapter 11.

CHURCH AND STATE

To understand the principle of ecclesiastical sanctuary, let us look at two historic events. The first we shall consider happened in 1983 in Louisville, Nebraska. The state of Nebraska decided that Faith Baptist Church should not be permitted to run a Christian school because it was "unlicensed." Officers of the state attempted to shut down the school, and in response, hundreds of clergymen came to Louisville from all over the United States. Determined to shut down the school, the sheriff of Cass County, Nebraska, and his troopers invaded a prayer meeting at the church, forcibly hauled out the praying pastors, and padlocked the doors of the church. (So much for separation of church and state in Nebraska in 1983.)

In January, A. D. 532, there was a riot in the Hippodrome in Constantinople. (The Hippodrome was Constantinople's Colosseum.) The riot was a minor one, but those involved were protesting the tax policies of the Emperor Justinian, ruler of the entire Roman world. A few men were tried and sentenced to be hanged. At the execution, the ropes hanging two of the men broke as they dropped from the scaffold. Undaunted, the hangman obtained a second rope and tried again. Again the rope broke, and the men fell to the ground. The sympathetic crowd surged forward, taking these events as a sign from God, and bore the two men to the Church of Saint Lawrence, where they were granted sanctuary.

The Emperor Justinian did not dare to order the arrest of the two tax rebels as long as they remained in the safety of the house of God, under the protection of the Church. Though his soldiers stood guard to catch them if they came out, no soldier dared enter the church.

But what Roman soldiers once dared not do, local sheriffs and American policemen are now ready to do without qualm. What Emperors once avoided is now carried out with impunity by gun-slinging "lawmen" in small American towns.

The Christian Church maintains that "wherever two or three are gathered" in Jesus' name, He is present with them. In ancient Israel, God's presence formed a sanctuary around His throne. So it is in the Church as well. During worship, heaven is open, and the church becomes God's sanctuary. This is like the sanctuary of the altar or temple in the Old Testament. During the rest of the week, the property of the church is to be regarded as a sanctuary, even though worship is not taking place. This is like the sanctuary of the cities of refuge in the Old Testament.

It took a great deal of effort for Christianity to establish the right of sanctuary in Western civilization. Broadly speaking, the right of sanctuary specifies the *institutional distinction between church and state as well as their independent integrity*. Narrowly speaking, it means that armed officers of the state may never enter the premises of the church to capture a criminal who has been granted refuge. In the narrow sense, the right of sanctuary is totally ignored in the United States today, and increasingly the separation of church and state is also ignored, as the state taxes Church property and seeks to take over Church schools.

Secular societies, whether neo-pagan (humanist) or paleo-pagan, have no right of sanctuary. There is only one government, the state, and that government has total rights over every area of life. There was no separation of Church and state in the Soviet Union; rather, the Church (as a governmental institution) was completely controlled by the civil rulers. The United States has been moving in this same direction in recent years.

When the civil magistrate recognizes the Church's right of sanctuary, however, then clearly the tyranny of the state has been broken. The magistrate recognizes the existence of a separate government, visible on the earth, with a separate jurisdiction. He also acknowledges a geographical area, a place, beyond which his power—that of the state's sword—cannot go unless invited.

The importance of this fact to our discussion is this: As Christians we are concerned with *discipling the nations*. We have seen that the pagan/humanist state tends to crush the nations through tyranny, shuffling of populations, irrelevant boundary lines, and the like. The pagan/humanist view places the importance of the state above the nations. By contrast, we have seen that Christian localism makes the state relatively small and magnifies the nations as the organic branches of humanity. By breaking the monolithic tyranny of the civil ruler, the right of sanctuary works to free the nations and peoples from bondage.

By limiting the power of the civil ruler, the right of sanctuary opens up other areas of freedom. As historian Brian Tierney has put it, in Western civilization, "the very existence of two power structures competing for men's allegiance instead of only one compelling obedience greatly enhanced the possibilities for human freedom."[76] This enables the nations to flower in Godliness and obviously makes for common international community, peace, and good relations.

The right of sanctuary also serves to establish within each nation a truly international community: the Church. The Bible says that in the Lord's Day when we gather with other Christians to worship we are mystically in the presence of all the angels, the departed saints, and all other Christians in the world (Heb. 12:18-24). We don't *see* all these other saints and angels, nor can we *talk* to them, but there is a sense in which they are all present together, because we are present with Jesus Christ and He is present with all of the rest. This is the sense of international community in and through Christ that the Church cultivates in her prayers "for the whole estate of Christ's Church" and in her world-missions programs.

When the Church is oppressed, and meets in hiding, then the right of sanctuary is not recognized. When the civil magistrates recognize the right of sanctuary, however, they are thereby also recognizing that the Church is a true international community. The more effective the influence of this international community becomes, the more world peace will develop and true international relations flower.

POLITICAL SANCTUARY AND THE NATIONS

As we just noted, the right of sanctuary established and sealed in a visible way the separation of Church and state. It guaranteed two separate court systems. Beyond that, however, it created the possibility for more systems of law courts in society. After all, if there are two separate court

---

76 Brian Tierney, *The Crisis of Church and State: 1050-1300* (Englewood Cliffs, N.J.: Prentice-Hall, 1964), 2.

systems, each with its own proper task, why not more? In other words, why should society by unified by the *state*, by the civil rulers?

Rushdoony has pointed out that this Christian idea of multiple courts is the heart of *feudalism* and that the heart of protestant social theory was a restoration and purification of Christian feudalism.[77] Rushdoony summarizes the situation:

> Under paganism each religio-political entity or order had one total law. Under feudalism, a variety of laws governing various areas became the order of the day and was pushed to its limits. There was village law, fief law.... church or canon law, Roman law, law of the merchants, Jewish law, and so on. Law was thus class and sphere law, and sometimes contract law. A great variety of courts and jurisdictions existed, each strictly limited in its sway. The modern conception of state law, total in its scope and jurisdiction, was thus alien to feudalism.[78]

This fact of Christian feudalism or localism opens the possibility of "ghettoes" or zones of local law and custom within a larger society. It opens the possibility for small local nations and peoples to exist within larger governments with their local law systems preserved. It can be seen that such "ghettoes" are like sanctuaries.

Christian nations have even permitted such sanctuaries for non-Christian religions, provided the devotees of such religions do not try to overthrow the wider Christian social order. In a sense, such true "pluralism" is possible only

---

77 This is the thesis of Rushdoony's book, *This Independent Republic* (Fairfax, Va.: Thoburn Press, [1964] 1978). The particular essay to which I make reference is Chapter 2: "Feudalism and Federalism."

78 Ibid., 11.
For a full discussion of the boundaries between church and state courts, and other law-court systems, see Harold J. Berman, *Law and Revolution: The Formation of the Western Legal Tradition* (Cambridge, Mass.: Harvard University Press, 1983).

where the Christian doctrine of sanctuary is established. Non-Christian societies are never truly pluralistic. Pagan Rome would not tolerate Christianity at all, and neither do consistent Islamic nations today. In the United States today, the intolerant religion of secular humanism threatens to destroy all Christian institutions through regulation and taxation, as numerous Christian school court cases demonstrate.

Another implication of the concept of sanctuary is this: It opens up the possibility for one nation to have a sanctuary within another, such as an embassy. Such embassies could facilitate international travel, international study, and the protection of traders and missionaries.

Let us discuss a couple of possibilities. Friendly nations might exchange embassies to facilitate travel and cultural exchanges. Mr. and Mrs. Jones make a trip to England, a friendly nation. If the Joneses get into trouble, they can call upon the American Embassy to help them.

Another possibility is this: A Christian nation is attacked by a pagan neighbor. The Christian nation is victorious, and part of the terms of surrender is that the Christian nation will be allowed an embassy in the pagan nation. This embassy will act to protect missionaries and traders that the Christian nation sends into the pagan nation.

Should ambassadors and other national representatives be given "diplomatic immunity? I think it all depends on what is meant by this. In some ways, an embassy should be a sanctuary for the ambassador and his staff, freeing them from local customs and laws that have nothing to do with them. On the other hand, diplomatic immunity should not mean that diplomats can flout local law with impunity. If a diplomat or ambassador refuses to obey speed limits, he should be fined the same as anyone else and deported if his behavior does not improve. Such limits of sanctuary should be spelled out in the agreements that establish the embassy.

CONCLUSION

When God places His Name in a particular place, a sanctuary is established. Ultimately, the idea of sanctuary comes from the special place God establishes around His throne. Historically, the Christian church has insisted that the place where worship is conducted on earth before God's throne should be regarded as a sanctuary for the oppressed. Additionally, the church has always claimed that her sanctuary property is to be recognized as such by the civil rulers, and neither taxed nor invaded. This right of sanctuary establishes the church as a separate jurisdiction with separate courts. By extension, Christian societies have many court systems and a highly diversified and decentralized legal system, called feudalism or localism. Also, within a Christian society, there may be local areas that preserve local laws and customs—a true pluralism. Finally, the right of sanctuary means that individual nations recognize the transcendent and international character of the church, and makes for good and creative international relations. The church can often act as a mediator in disputes, when she is thus recognized. By extension, political sanctuaries can exist as one nation maintains a sanctuary, consulate, or embassy within another.

The Sanctuary Movement and the Immigration Problem

Each will be like a refuge from the wind and a shelter from the storm, like streams of water in a dry country, like the shade of a huge rock in an exhausted land.
 — Isa. 32:2 (New American Standard Bible)

The problem of immigration and the associated Sanctuary Movement is an increasingly visible one in the United States today. In the debate are two major camps. One is comprised mainly of liberal humanists, including liberal churchmen, who hold a pro-leftist, anti-American viewpoint on Central American affairs, and who use biblical and historic arguments to put forth a case in favor of free immigration.[79] The other camp is made up of certain conservatives who

---

79 Gary MacEoin, ed., *Sanctuary: A Resource Guide for Understanding and Participating in the Central American Refugees' Struggle* (San Francisco, Calif.: Harper & Row, 1985).

see numerous problems with unrestricted immigration and who call for strict enforcement of anti-immigration laws. Not all conservatives oppose free immigration, however.

An extreme alternative would be this: No state has the right to tell people where they may or may not live, except on a religious basis. The earth is the Lord's, and He has given it to men, not to the state. Men should be free to move anywhere they wish and live anywhere they please.

The problem with this position is that it fails to take into account that God has organized men into nations, and has determined their boundaries (Acts 17:26). God does desire there to be many nations and cultures, each glorifying Him in its own unique ways. Thus, a totally homogenous view of humanity—people moving here and there without respect for culture and tradition—is a non-Christian abstraction.

Why would anyone want to move away from his nation—remembering that the nations are pretty small, local groups—and go live among foreigners? Well, perhaps for education, or for business. Such moves are generally temporary, however, and seldom involve enough people to cause any difficulty.

No, the real problem comes with refugees. The people who flooded to America's shores during the past two centuries were refugees: refugees from tyrannies of one sort or another. The United States of America became, as a nation, a sanctuary for refugees. The entire nation was a city of refuge for the world. This makes the United States unique among nations, and is an important part of our heritage.

Israel of old was also to be a sanctuary to the world, and thus there are principles in the Old Testament law that can form a useful starting point for acquiring wisdom for America today.

THE BIBLICAL POSITION

As we saw in Chapter 10, the Bible teaches that a Christian nation is to give refuge to the oppressed. No one fleeing to us is to be denied sanctuary. There are, however, two stipulations that we did not look at in Chapter 10 and that we must now consider.

First of all, the resident alien was not permitted to continue to worship his pagan gods. He was required to break his idols at the gate, so to speak. He was seeking sanctuary from the God of Israel, and he had to acknowledge Yahweh as his Protector, even if he did not come to saving faith. If he wanted the protection of Israel's laws, he had to obey them. Among those laws was this:

> If you hear in one of your cities, which Yahweh your God is giving you to live in, anyone saying that some worthless men have gone out from among you and have seduced the inhabitants of their city, saying, "Let's go and serve other gods" (whom you have not known), then you shall investigate, search out, and inquire thoroughly. And if it is true and the matter is certain that this abomination has been committed among you, you shall most certainly strike the inhabitants of that city with the edge of the sword. Utterly destroy it and all who are in it and its cattle, with the edge of the sword. (Deut. 13:12-15, NASB)

It is noteworthy that this law is phrased in terms of the city, for that was where resident aliens were permitted to live. The same language is found in Deut. 17:1-5. This law applied to all, not just to the Israelite, because, "There shall be only one standard for you; it shall be for the stranger as well as the native, for I am Yahweh your God" (Lev. 24:22, NASB).

Thus, some form of *external, social conversion* was required of anyone seeking sanctuary. He did not have attend synagogue. He did not have to "join a church." But he did have to give external lip service to the God under whose wings he was seeking refuge.

In the early 19th century, when one boatload after another of immigrants came to the United States, they were met by Christian workers. They were given clothing, shelter, and work. They were evangelized. In this way, the principle of conversion was practically worked out, and it was the Church that did it.

Second, refugees did not immediately become citizens of Israel. Depending on where they came from, it might take a long time for them to be admitted. "No Ammonite or Moabite may enter the assembly of the Lord; none of their descendants, even to the tenth generation..." (Deut. 23:3, NASB). On the other hand, "You shall not loathe an Edomite, for he is your brother; you shall not loathe an Egyptian, because you were a stranger in his land. The sons of the third generation who are born to them may enter the assembly of Yahweh" (Deut. 23:7-8, ESV).

Now, these laws had a particular meaning for Israel that they do not have for us. To "enter the assembly" meant to be circumcised and to become an Israelite. Not all converts were circumcised, for there were God-fearing Gentiles in the ancient world, and many lived in the cities of the Israelites. All the same, the law stated that even circumcised converts were not permitted to take up the responsibilities of full citizenship—leadership in the synagogue and voting in national affairs—until several generations had gone by. They had to become acculturated to the ways of the Israelite nation before they could presume to take up any kind of leadership.

The outpouring of the Holy Spirit does grant greater power to the Church in the New Testament, and history moves faster as a result. Perhaps we should not ask people to wait three whole generations before they are allowed to vote, but a good long wait is entirely Scriptural—say a Jubilee period of 50 years? It takes more than seven years to learn English, learn our laws and customs, and become integrated into our life.

In Israel, immigrants and refugees could not live in the land, because the land reverted to its Jewish owners in the Jubilee year. Rather, refugees lived in the cities. We are not bound to this Old Testament law any longer, because we have no Jubilee and no allotted lands. There is, however, an important principle bound up in this distinction.

Would it be proper or wise for an established nation, such as Wales, to allow itself to become swamped by hordes of refugees? This is a problem in Great Britain today, because so many Moslems have moved there. Such a massive influx of aliens can destroy the culture and traditions of the existing nation, and in my opinion that would be a bad thing. God does not want the distinctive beauties of any nation to be swamped. At the same time, compassion and biblical principles dictate that some provision be made for refugees. Setting aside certain areas, analogous to the cities in ancient Israel, would be a way to solve this problem. The lands set aside would be sanctuaries—ghettoes in the older sense of the term—in which refugees might live and continue their own customs.

The situation in the United States is completely different. The Statue of Liberty, newly refurbished, stands to remind us that our whole nation is a nation of refugees, from the Pilgrims and Puritans to the Boat People of Indo-China. We are one vast sanctuary, and we have a special place and privilege among the nations of the world. There is no reason for us to give up this special heritage and calling. With this in mind, let us turn to the current problems in the area of immigration.

"America is being invaded," is the opening line in an inflammatory anti-immigration paperback published by The American Immigration Control Foundation.[80] Replete with charts, graphs, projections, and lots of rhetoric, this volume is an unfortunate example of the way people who think of themselves as conservatives try to use traditional liberal arguments to win their case.

Let's examine their position.

JOB ROBBERS!

The authors of the American Immigration Control Foundation publication claim that immigrants—refugees from tyranny and socialism—take away jobs that "belong" to Americans (Chapter 9, "Importing Unemployment"). Against this contention, we can make several observations.

First, new immigrants work for less and take jobs that established Americans don't want to do. At least this was the case until the minimum wage law came along. The minimum wage law prices the lower classes out of the market and creates unemployment. "At least three million idle Americans owe their unemployment to this labor law. Teenagers and uneducated, unskilled minority workers are its primary victims."[81] But this has nothing to do with immigration. The solution: Repeal the minimum wage law, or at least (as a start) make an exception for refugees.

---

80 G. Palmer Stacy III and Wayne Lutton, Ph.D., *The Immigration Time Bomb* (Alexandria, Va.: 1985), vii.

81 Hans Sennholz, *Age of Inflation* (Belmont, Mass.: Western Islands, 1979), 155.

Second, it is argued that automation is throwing Americans out of work, and immigrants only make the situation worse. This argument has been around for 200 years. It is not true. Automation creates as many jobs as it relieves. Two centuries of continuing advances in automation proves it. Now, if in fact automation destroys jobs, then the problem is not immigration but automation. Let's destroy the machines, they may cry. But where is the evidence that automation causes more than very temporary unemployment? There is no such evidence.

Third, it is not the business of the "haves" (wealthy Americans with jobs) to use the power of the state to abuse the "have nots" (poor refugees). That is nothing but tyranny and socialism of the very worst sort. How can people consider themselves "conservatives" and advocate such immorality?

Fourth, these new workers are here to work. By taking jobs at the bottom of the ladder, they increase productivity, freeing up other workers from these less desirable jobs. By increasing the labor force, they increase the number of middle management jobs, jobs for established Americans. You can't go up the ladder if there is no one to replace you in the job you left behind.

POPULATION EXPLODERS!

The authors of this book devote their Chapter 4 to "The World Population Explosion." Here is more liberal goop served up as if it were "conservative" thought. There is in fact no such thing as a population explosion, as has been pointed out by sensible researchers.[82]

---

82 For instance, Robert L. Sassone, *Handbook on Population* (Sanata Ana, Calif., 1973); James A. Weber, *Grow or Die!* (New Rochelle, N.Y.: Arlington House, 1977); Colin Clark, *Population Growth: The Advantages* (Santa Ana, Calif., 1972); Julian L. Simon, *The Ultimate Resource* (Princeton, N.J.: Princeton University Press, 1981); and finally Rousas J. Rushdoony,

Moreover, the Bible repeatedly presents population growth as desirable (Gen. 1:28; 9:1, 7; Lev. 26:9; Deut. 28:4, 11)—at least for the Godly.[83]

These authors want to paint a picture of masses of Latin Americans swarming into our already-packed United States. But anyone who has ever driven across country knows that vast reaches of the United States are unpopulated and are just waiting for Godly people to move in and take dominion.

Overpopulation is not an issue.

LEECHES!

In a chapter called "Aliens Raid the Welfare System," the authors provide evidence that some illegal aliens are taking advantage of the welfare system in the United States. Surprise, surprise. So are loads of Americans.

It is certainly understandable that poor people in Latin America look to the United States as a land of plenty and take advantage of welfare when they get here. The problem is not with *them*; the problem is with the modern welfare system. Let government bureaucrats get out of the welfare business, and let the Church get back into it.[84]

The Myth of Overpopulation (Nutley, N.J.: The Craig Press, 1969).

83 On this see Gary North, *Moses and Pharaoh* (Tyler, Tex.: Institute for Christian Economics, 1985), Chapter 1; and Chilton, *Productive Christians*, Chapter 7.

84 On welfarism and its problems, see David Chilton's book mentioned above, and George Grant, *Bringing in the Sheaves: Transforming Poverty into Productivity* (Atlanta, Ga.: American Vision, 1985).

CRIMINALS!

In their chapter "The Alien Crime Wave," the authors point out that lots of criminals are included among refugees. True. Criminals, however, have a way of ignoring anti-immigration laws, just as they ignore other laws. The maxim that "when guns are outlawed, only outlaws will have guns" applies to other situations as well: When immigration is outlawed, only outlaws will be immigrants.

We would be a lot better off to welcome everyone who wants to come in. Such a population mix would police its own criminal elements better than established Americans can.

Moreover, the obvious answer to this problem is to reform our justice system and bring it into conformity with Christian law.

Criminals should be tried speedily, punished properly, and thus dealt with. Nowadays all criminals, local or alien, are coddled. The problem is not with immigrants, but with our own perverted "justice" system.

But there is another kind of bad guy "sneaking into America." Our authors tell us that if we let everyone in, we are issuing an "Invitation to Terrorism and Subversion" (Chapter 12 of their book). Well, let's examine this.

First, it is true that many communists and subversives will try to come into the United States if our borders are open. It is also true that they are already coming in, because they are criminals. Closing our borders will not stop them. Closing our borders will only hurt the honest poor.

Second, if our nation used Christian principles, it would require a pledge of allegiance to the laws of the Bible and to the United States from all those seeking refuge in our land. If a man were a known communist (worshiper of an alien god), he might be excluded or at least evangelized more heavily than others.

Third, the fact is that after a while many such subversives are converted to the American way after they have lived here. Let me recall my college days, if I may, and describe a situation that is similar. I was at the University of Georgia from 1967 to 1971, the heyday of the Students for a Democratic Society. The SDS was made up largely of spoiled brats, rich kids with guilt complexes who didn't want to go to Vietnam and who wanted to salve their consciences by identifying with the poor and downtrodden. There was another group that often marched with the SDS: the Black Student Union. Now, many conservatives made the mistake of thinking that these young blacks were a "bunch of commies" just like the SDS brats, but they were wrong. The blacks were actually interested in becoming part of the system, but they were frustrated. Their frustration was enhanced, of course, by manipulation from the leftist media. All in all, however, their basic motivation was a desire to participate in the American good life. This was a very different basic motivation from that of the rich SDS kids.

The same thing is true of many Latin American "leftists." Once they get here and begin to enjoy the good life, they curiously lose their ideological commitments. It is one thing to hate the United States when you are living in squalor in the home country. It is hard to keep up the hate once you begin to do all right in the new country. Prosperity has a way of blunting ideological fervor among the poor.

Subversion is a problem for an unhealthy society, and our society is unhealthy in some ways. The answer, however, is not immigration laws but a revival of Christianity. A healthy society cannot be subverted.

Most refugees want a good life in America. Very few want to subvert that good life. They will police their own, never fear. The worst enemy of a Hispanic subversive is a loyal Hispanic American. Let's help them be loyal by allowing them to bring their families and friends to the good land.

PLAGUE!

The last threat our authors raise to scare us is the promise of disease: "The Alien Health Threat." Yes, it's true, people who move to the United States from less well developed nations can bring diseases with them.

So inoculate them at the border. As long as immigration is so largely restricted, aliens will sneak across at places other than border checkpoints, bringing diseases with them. Therefore again, the most reasonable way to deal with the problem is to allow them entry, but inoculate them as they come in.

SUMMATION

The authors of the American Immigration Control Foundation publication want a whole series of statist solutions to the problem of immigration. They want to increase taxes to provide for a massive army to keep refugees out of our land. Gary North reports that Senator Simpson of Wyoming has introduced a bill to issue "worker identity cards," which every person must show to an employer before being hired. North comments, "in terms of lost civil liberties and the growth of Federal bureaucratic power, a National Identity Card would be a national disaster. It sounds like something out of Nazi-controlled Europe or the Soviet Union today."[85] Such is the statist solution.

North summarizes the Christian solution:

> What should be done about illegal aliens? First, require

---

85 Gary North, *The Last Train Out* (Fort Worth, Tex.: American Bureau of Economic Research, 1983), 132.

> proof of immunization, or require those without proof to be immunized. Second, abolish the minimum wage law. Third, abolish all public welfare programs. Fourth, abolish the requirement that the children of illegal aliens be required to attend public schools at taxpayers' expense. Just let them work, at whatever wage they can get. In short, let them enjoy the freedom that we all want.[86]

In fact, abolish all immigration quotas and restrictions so that there are no more "illegal" aliens. After all, immigrants are not "illegal" except when our government tries to say they are. They are not "illegal" in God's eyes or in the eyes of Christian people.

We fixed up the Statue of Liberty in 1986. Let her remind us of our privilege and calling. Let us not turn away any more boat people. Let us not turn away any more suffering Latin Americans. Let us welcome them as human brethren and Christianize them. Let us get the Church to work and make new men and women of them, as our forefathers did.

THE SANCTUARY MOVEMENT

The Sanctuary Movement in the United States is a mixed bag. Some people are involved in it out of compassion and a desire to help. Others are involved because they are anti-American leftists who want to "stick it to the government." Still others are doubtless conspiratorial communists who want to help bring subversives into our land.

The present Sanctuary Movement does not seem interested in helping refugees from communist countries. As Duke Austin of the Immigration and Naturalization Services put it:

> The test of the sanctuary movement is: They make sure that those individuals they bring in are very articulate in

---

86 Idem.

speaking out against U.S. policy in Central America. They have never, *never*, accepted anyone fleeing (Communist-backed) Nicaragua. And if you're fleeing Guatemala or El Salvador and you still speak out in favor of those governments, they don't want anything to do with you.

Identical complaints have come from Maria Thomas of the Institute on Religion and Democracy and Bishop Rene Gracida of the Corpus Christi Diocese in Texas.[87]

In spite of this, the Sanctuary Movement gets lots of press, and virtually all of it is good press. Even when they are criticized they come off smelling like roses. After all, they are putting themselves at considerable risk to help the poor. It is hard to criticize them without looking like demons by comparison.

How should our rulers deal with the Sanctuary Movement? Should they infiltrate it? Should they crush it? Should they pass laws allowing the United States government to invade churches to remove refugees?

There is a better solution: Open our borders. The Sanctuary Movement would not be necessary and would die. There would be no more good press for leftist agitators to use. The United States would come off smelling like a rose.

CONCLUSION

The assumption of "closed border conservatives" is that Christianity doesn't work, that Christianity cannot convert large numbers of immigrants. As Christians, we don't believe that. While many of the fears of the "closed border conservative" have some validity, the position he winds up espousing is cruel, unreasonable, and impractical.

---

[87] Austin's statement, and statements from Thomas and Gracida, are from an article, "Sanctuary Movement: The Hidden Agenda in Smuggling Aliens," *Fundamentalist Journal 5:9* (October, 1986), 61.

Cruel because it hurts the poor. Unreasonable because it hurts American economic life. And impractical because it virtually requires that a "Berlin Wall" be build along our southern borders. The Christian has a better alternative to offer.

A Christian Foreign Polity

Go, therefore, and make disciples of all the nations, baptizing them in the name of the Father and the Son and the Holy Spirit, teaching them to follow all that I commanded you; and behold, I am with you always, to the end of the age.
— Matt. 28:19-20 (New American Standard Version)

Throughout this study we have maintained three points. First is that the *integrity* of each nation is safeguarded by its boundaries, its language, customs, and traditions, and its local governments.

Second is that the *unity* of all nations is to be found only in the Christian faith, arising out of the life of the Church, which is the nursery of the nations. And third is that the *interactions* of the nations are primarily in the area of trade (goods, arts, ideas): free trade protected by Christian law.

In this final chapter, we want to look briefly at the two major prongs of a Christian foreign policy. The foundational prong is *world missions and a united Church*. The secondary prong is *free trade*. We begin with trade, and will close our study with a look at the Church and what you and I can do to improve true international relations.

FREE TRADE

Throughout our study, we have maintained that it is cruel and immoral for the "haves" to use the power of the state to oppress the "have nots" or to protect themselves from competition from the poor. Historically, of course, once people come to power, they use that power for just such evil purposes. They erect immigration barriers to keep away the poor. They create "closed shop" labor unions to prevent poor people from taking away their jobs by working for less. They pass "minimum wage laws" to protect themselves and to price poor people out of the market. They create a "myth of overpopulation" in order to justify a campaign of sterilization against the black, brown, and yellow peoples of the world.

And they erect tariffs.

David Chilton provides a succinct discussion of tariffs, what they are, and why they are wrong. He writes that tariffs...

> ...are protective barriers to trade which a country erects in order to guard its own industries from external competition. The idea is that, for example, our television manufacturers will lose their jobs if cheaper and better sets from Japan are available to the American consumers. The American people will stop buying the more expensive American-made TVs in favor of the imported ones. This will mean fewer jobs in the TV industry, and hence rising unemployment and poverty in our country. Thus, to protect our people, we force importers to pay a tax on their manufactures, which will raise the price of their goods to a level at which our own industries can successfully compete....This is merely a bundle of

fallacies. First, a tariff is theft, since it confiscates the property of others ('strangers,' among others [by which Chilton means the 'stranger in the land,' who is to be protected by the law and not exploited, according to the Bible—JBJ]) in the name of protection for ourselves. Breaking God's law will lead to national judgment, not higher employment.

Second, it steals from the consumers, who are forced to pay higher prices for goods, and must therefore reduce their spending on other products if they wish to buy a 'protected' item.

Third, it turns trade into warfare, regarding foreign producers as enemies against whom we must defend ourselves—thus creating, not free competition, but a dangerous conflict (which has historically led to actual war again and again).

Fourth, it does not keep Americans employed. The tariff adds to consumer cost, and many will forego the purchase of any TV, which will bring about unemployment in the industry anyway.

Fifth, it subsidizes inefficiency by prohibiting competition. Free trade means that a producer must strive constantly to make his product better or cheaper than those of his competitors. Free trade presents consumers with goods that are continually improving.

Sixth, free trade does not ultimately produce unemployment at all. The less efficient producers will be forced out of a market in which they are doing poorly; but they will then turn their energies toward manufactures which they can produce well—and the consumer, having saved money from the lower cost of the Japanese TV, will be able to spend whatever is left over on another item. Also, Japanese buyers can now use American dollars to buy American products—soybeans,

> for example, or lumber. The same amount of money is spent—but now with more efficiency, greater diversity, higher productivity, no theft, and no warlike activity on the part of the state.[88]

It is clear that everyone benefits from free trade. The temporary dislocations that can be caused by free trade are nothing in comparison with the massive dislocations caused by an artificially protected economy.

Is it ever right for a nation to interfere with free trade? Yes, in time of war. Since free trade is a blessing, it is important to withhold its benefits from those who wish to destroy us. Trade with the enemy simply builds him up and enables him to kill more people.

Here again we have to reflect on the Cold War situation. The Soviet Union made it clear that it was at war with the entire Christian West. The U.S.S.R. acted consistently to undermine and defeat the other countries of the world. Should we permit free trade with the Soviet Union, when Lenin publicly remarked that "the West will gladly sell us the rope that we will use to hang them"?

The fact is that the economic and military development of the Soviet Union was due almost entirely to Western technology. American corporations have gladly sold our best technology to our declared enemies.[89] Moreover, when we sold grain to the Soviets, especially at taxpayer-financed reduced prices, this enabled them to put their money into more war material.

It could be argued that if we sell to France, then France will sell to the Soviets. Maybe, but there will be an extra cost to pay for the middle man—the French will add carrying

---

88 Chilton, *Productive Christians*, 101-102; some paragraph breaks added. Chilton calls attention to W. M. Curtiss, *The Tariff Idea* (New York, N.Y.: Irvington-on-Hudson, The Foundation for Economic Education, 1953).

89 See Antony C. Sutton, *Western Technology and Soviet Economic Development*, 3 volumes (Stanford, Calif.: Hoover Institution, 1968, 1971, 1973).

charges. Of course, the Cold War is only a partial conflict, and there can be some give and take in our policies. The principle, however, is that you do not give "most favored" trade status to those who are sworn to destroy you.

Another problem occurs when a nation, like China, heavily subsidizes its own production as a national policy of economic war against other nations. Over a long span of time, this can be a genuinely debilitating assault on free trade. Arguably a nation can protect itself by tariffs in such a case, but from a biblical point of view, such tariffs should only serve to restore a free and equal market place, not as a means of economic war against, say, China.

"When goods do not cross borders, armies will." This statement is attributed to Frederick Bastiat. Wherever it is from, it is true.

FREE SEAS

Free trade cannot take place apart from free seas. There are three questions of international relations that concern us here: boundary, war, and piracy.

How far out to sea does the jurisdiction of a nation extend? How close to our shores do we let *their* fishing boats come? These are legitimate questions, and they are questions of boundary. We have seen that it is legitimate for nations to create treaties to define boundaries. A three-mile or fifteen-mile limit is a reasonable boundary, for instance. (A mile is 1.60934 kilometers, for those who need such information.)

What if a nation insists on a 200-mile limit? Do we have to respect it? There is no biblical principle that says we must. The tradition in "international law" is that such ocean boundaries are as good as the power of the nation claiming them. If a nation can actually *enforce* a 200-mile limit, then there is no point in crossing it. If the 200-mile limit is only a fiction, then other nations are free to ignore it and keep to the agreed-upon standard of, say, fifteen miles.

What about nations that seek to restrict the freedom of the seas? The Soviet Union sought to dominate and control the so-called "choke points" of the world. If the Soviet Union were a fellow Christian nation, some international agreement might be reached regarding freedom of the seas. As it is, however, the Soviet Union is at Cold War with the United States and with the rest of the Christian (or residually Christian) world. It is perfectly legitimate for the United States and other nations to defend the seas against the warmongering encroachments of the Soviet fleet.

Most of such responsibility will naturally fall upon the United States, but that is simply our place and responsibility in the community of nations. If we protect the weak, that is to our good.

Some have advocated that merchants hire private navies to protect themselves. In some situations, that may be necessary, but from a Christian standpoint, God has given the sword to the civil magistrate, not to private citizens or private enterprise. Our Navy should act to protect our trade, financed by legitimate taxation.

Moreover, modern military technology is so devastating that it can hardly be sold to private enforcers. The maintenance of the sword is unquestionably a state function today.

Finally, piracy. Christian nations have frequently joined hands to war against piracy. At other times, one or another nation has taken on pirates directly, as the United States did in the case of the Barbary pirates in the early 1800s. As we have seen, the Knights Hospitallers worked to keep the Mediterranean Sea free of Arab pirates for two centuries, acting as a navy delegated by the European nations. Free seas are essential for free trade, and it is perfectly legitimate for a nation to protect the seas from pirates and from warmongers.

THE CHURCH

As Christians, we are interested in discipling the nations and in working for a Christian world. Christians' opinions differ among themselves as to how much they expect to see happen before Christ returns, but all can agree that we must now be about the Father's business.

The nations will not be discipled, however, until the Church is reformed. While there is much work to be done in shaping up the life and doctrine of the churches, the main point we need to look at here is the matter of cooperation and Church union.

We have seen that the Church is always truly united in her Head, Jesus Christ. Sadly, men do not always treat the Church as united. Doctrinal differences, differences of custom and tradition, and sinful pride all conspire to separate the churches one from another.

There is no particular reason, however, why all the churches on the earth need to be in one monolithic governmental body. Each church has Christ as her Head, after all. The proper unity of the churches needs to come through *mutual respect and recognition*.

If we look at the New Testament, we see local churches in a variety of conditions. The church at Philippi was in much better spiritual shape than the church in Corinth, at least at the time of Paul's first letter to Corinth. We can look at Revelation 2 and 3 to see a real variety of churches, some afflicted with gross heresies in their midst. Yet, all these were true churches. They were expected to stand together.

Modern protestant churches generally do not "recognize" one another, however. Various denominations work to create "fraternal relations" with some, while denying such "fraternal relations" to others.

The fact is, however, that any church that professes Christ as sole Savior, worships the Trinity, and administers baptism and the Lord's Supper is a true church. It may be the Church at Sardis—weak, full of error, threatened with extinction—but it is still the church. Christ is still her Lord and King. The Church at Sardis is still the Bride of Christ, and we are not to despise her weakness but help and pray for her.

In view of these facts, churches can and should recognize one another. This means two things, practically. First, members should not be allowed to move from one church to another without letters of transfer. If a man comes to my church from yours, we will not receive him without contacting you to see about the matter. If the churches would treat one another honorably like this, it would make for peace and unity and would set an example for the nations.

Second, churches must respect one another's discipline. If a man has been excommunicated or banned from a local church, he has been banned from all churches. He should not be received into another church unless he goes and makes it right with the church that disciplined him. In the case of false and evil discipline, a third church should be asked to examine and pronounce on the matter.

In this way, the churches can accord one another mutual respect as joint heirs of the grace of life. If the churches would learn cooperation and unity, then they could disciple the nations.

What about real doctrinal differences? Should we just ignore or downplay these? Not at all. There can be no reformation without truth. The issues need to be made visible and be actively debated. Such a commitment to integrity does not, however, mean we cannot have a true biblical catholicity as well.[90]

The Church is the nursery of the nations. When she shapes up, the nations will shape up. The principles of integrity and cooperation learned in the Church can be extended to the world, but judgment begins at the house of God. The world cannot be reformed unless the Church is reformed.

So, what can you and I do to help international relations? We can and must pray for all nations, of course. And we should support the international labor of missionaries. But we must also make every effort to build churches that cooperate with others without losing their distinctives. In that way, we build true unity and strength, and nothing will be withheld from us.

---

90 I have discussed this at greater length, and with practical suggestions, in my book, *The Sociology of the Church*, 11ff.

Bibliography

Barnes, Harry Elmer. *The Genesis of the World War*. Alfred A. Knopf, 1926.

Berman, Harold J. *Law and Revolution: The Formation of the Western Legal Tradition*. Cambridge, Mass.: Harvard University Press, 1983.

Bradford, Ernle. *The Shield and the Sword: The Knights of St. John, Jerusalem, Rhodes, and Malta*. New York, N.Y.: E. P. Dutton, 1973.

Chilton, David. *Productive Christians in an Age of Guilt-Manipulators*. Third edition; Tyler, Tex.: The Institute for Christian Economics, 1985.

Dawson, Christopher. *The Judgment of the Nations*. New York, N.Y.: Sheed and Ward, 1942.

Eliot, T. S. *Christianity and Culture*. New York, N.Y.: Harcourt, Brace, and World, 1949.

Johnson, Paul. *Modern Times: The World from the Twenties to the Eighties*. New York, N.Y.: Harper and Row, 1983.

Jordan, James B. *Judges: God's War Against Humanism*. Tyler, Tex.: Geneva Ministries, 1985.

_____. *The Sociology of the Church: Essays in Reconstruction*. Tyler, Tex.: Geneva Ministries, 1986.

Kwitty, Jonathan. *Endless Enemies: The Making of an Unfriendly World*. New York, N.Y.: Congdon and Weed, 1984.

Linebarger, Paul M. L. *Psychological Warfare*. New York, N.Y.: Duell, Sloan and Pierce, 1954.

North, Gary. *Conspiracy: A Biblical View*. Westchester, Ill.: Crossway Books, 1986.

Quigley, Carroll. *Tragedy and Hope: A History of the World in Our Time*. New York, N.Y.: Macmillan, 1966.

Roepke, Wilhelm. *Civitas Humana: A Humane Order of Society. Translated by Cyril Spencer Fox*. London: William Hodge and Company, 1948.

_____. *International Economic Disintegration*. London: William Hodge and Company, 1942.

Rushdoony, Rousas J. *The Nature of the American System*. Nutley, N.J.: The Craig Press, 1965.

_____. *The One and the Many*. Nutley, N.J.: The Craig Press, 1971.

_____. *This Independent Republic*. Nutley, N.J.: The Craig Press, 1964.

Tansill, Charles Callan. *America Goes to War*. Second edition; Boston, Mass.: Little, Brown, 1963.

Tierney, Brian. *The Crisis of Church and State: 1050-1300*. Englewood Cliffs, N.J.: Prentice-Hall, 1964.

Wines, E. C. *Commentaries on the Laws of the Hebrew Republic*. Philadelphia, Pa.: Presbyterian Board of Publication, 1853.

www.ingramcontent.com/pod-product-compliance
Lightning Source LLC
Chambersburg PA
CBHW050639300426
44112CB00012B/1867